BRAND *with* GRACE

ISBN: 979-8-9851550-5-1 (Paperback)

ISBN: 979-8-9851550-6-8 (ebook)

Cover design: Tech with Tasha

Book design: Lee Desmond

BRAND *with* GRACE

An Experience and Immersion Into Identity with God

**Uncover Your
True Kingdom
Identity**

Tasha Glover

Foreword

A brand is defined by the American Marketing Association, as a "name, term, design, symbol or any other feature that identifies one seller's goods or service as distinct from those of other seller's." When you're a Kingdom entrepreneur, the identity for your business, products, or services should be aligned with the mind and heart of King Jesus.

As Tasha's mentor, sister-in-Christ, and friend, I am a personal witness to the authentic and transformational fruit of her life and business journey. She carries sound wisdom and pure revelation that is rooted in scripture and saturated in her communion with God. The authentic way she teaches how to brand with God's empowering grace continuously leads to life-changing breakthroughs for those with ears to hear and a willingness to take Spirit-led action.

Brand With Grace is a gift that will help you uncover your true kingdom identity and mandate so you can show up and serve in the marketplace boldly and powerfully.

Don't simply read the following pages; embrace each invitation found within them. My prayer is that not only will you be encouraged, but by the power of Holy Spirit, your authentic brand will be both unlocked and unleashed!

Shae Bynes

Founder of Kingdom Driven Entrepreneur
Author of *Grace Over Grind* and *The Kingdom Driven Entrepreneur's Guide: Doing Business God's Way*

For Kenny

You are my greatest blessing. Thank you for your true love and wisdom that guide me through every step of my journey in uncovering my identity. I dedicate this book to you as a testament to the grace we share. I am honored to do life, family, business, and ministry with you.

Introduction

Growing up, like most children, I always had a curiosity about who I could become. I spent a lot of time in the library. I was consumed with choosing the best path for my life, and this started well before high school.

One of the books I would check out frequently was the *Occupational Outlook Handbook*. It had all the careers listed and the paths you needed to take to get there. I was always trying to figure out who I could be, thinking a career or education would finally give me the identity I was searching for.

I didn't realize it then, but that striving didn't disappear when I became an adult. It just matured.

I remember when I first started on this journey of discovering what God wanted me to do. There was a real freedom in knowing that I could be led by the Holy Spirit. But there was also conditioning I had become so accustomed to that I didn't recognize it right away within myself.

It was this: The things I could be led to do would always be in service of what someone else had created.

I could help others build **their** thing.
I could strengthen **their** structure.
I could improve **their** systems.

But I never saw the importance of being a vessel that God could flow His wisdom through for what He wanted to create **through me.**

That conditioning is normal, no matter what side of the track you grew up on. We're trained to climb someone else's ladder: to get the degree, to be the top executive in someone else's company. That's what gets applause. That's what feels stable. That's what we're told is consistent. And it's not necessarily wrong.

It's only an issue when you never learn to look upward and inward to discover what feels natural for you and how God designed you.

For me, it started as what I now call *holy curiosity*.

The ordinary started to feel wrong.
Unfair even.

Holy Curiosity and Holy Disruption

The nudging grew louder once I began having children. But the louder it got, the more I tried to reason myself back into what life was "supposed" to be.

Dropping my kids off in someone else's care for eight hours a day felt like bad parenting. And at work, I was bored. Deeply bored. My brain wasn't being fed. I would create memory games in my head just to stay engaged.

Ideas flooded me constantly—ways to improve systems, ways to increase productivity, ways to balance workload. I even thought about emailing the president of the company. But then fear would follow.

- What if they take my ideas and don't pay me?
- What if I look foolish?
- What in the world is wrong with me?

I talked to my husband about it over and over. We would circle the conversation but never land anywhere that felt peaceful. It all felt scary and big and disruptive. And honestly, I just wanted to be content. I wanted to be grateful. I wanted to settle.

But something was off.

And I didn't realize it then, but that unrest wasn't discontent. It was invitation.

My husband and I began talking more seriously about why I felt like that. I really felt like I was supposed to be at home. But it didn't make sense. I was the one making the most money. The kids were on my insurance. We would have to move things around. It wasn't convenient. It wasn't logical.

There had been little whispers before—at church, in thoughts about business. During maternity leave I would get all these ideas and start building things online. I didn't have anything concrete. I didn't have a real business. I had tried a couple of things before. Nothing stable. Nothing that looked like it could replace income.

Then one day in 2015, I had a dream. When I woke up from that dream, it was clear: I was going in the wrong direction.

I didn't fully know the timeline of how everything would happen. I just knew I couldn't ignore it. There was this fear that if I didn't respond, I would keep building something that didn't align with what God had for me. I hadn't even known I was on the wrong path before that. I just knew something was different. Something else was required of me.

I woke up and told my husband, "I'm supposed to quit my job and come home."

It wasn't strategic. It wasn't a two-week-notice plan. It felt like radical obedience.

I went to work intending to quit. I was crying so much I didn't even want to go into the building. I called my supervisor down to my car. She got in, and I looked at her and said, "I have to quit my job."

Even in that moment, I didn't have a business. I didn't have income lined up. I just had conviction.

She was shocked. But at the same time, she started telling me how she felt unappreciated there. And in this bold, almost crazy moment, I said, "When I start my business, I'll hire you."

Looking back, it sounds wild. It was a lot of emotions happening at once.

I didn't go back to work that Thursday.

By Sunday, I was being admitted into the hospital for my mental health. I ended up spending three days under observation.

It was one of the most disorienting seasons of my life.

Obedience, Faith, and Grace

I had stepped into obedience, but I didn't yet understand faith.

I didn't grow up in a Christian household, but I had been a Christian since my twenties. And I realized in that season that I didn't really know what it meant to trust God. I didn't know what walking by faith actually required.

After that, I did go back to work. I worked another nine months.

And then in April 2016, I officially left for good.

That was the real beginning.
Not the polished version.
Not the social media testimony.
The real beginning.

Learning how to hear God.
Learning how to discern between emotion and instruction.
Learning how to obey without collapsing.
Learning how to trust provision when I no longer controlled the paycheck.

Everything in this book was forged in that season.

At the time, I didn't have language for it. Now I understand: what I was bumping into, again and again, was **grace**.

- Grace that wouldn't let me stay in the wrong story.

- Grace that interrupted my plans and exposed my fears.

- Grace that invited me out of striving and into partnership.

- Grace that began to show me who I really was and what I was truly sent to do.

I eventually learned that my identity is not in any occupation—it is in what **God has graced me to be**.

Why This Book and Why Grace?

Through my journey, I realized that having a weak understanding of God leads to a false identity of self. Without a true perspective of who God is, you cannot know who you are. I was looking for my identity in church, in education, and in my career; but God showed me my kingdom identity, which is vast

and encompasses more than any worldly title or achievement. As He revealed Himself, He also revealed His grace on my life—what He had uniquely empowered me to do.
My calling is to help others discover their kingdom identity, and this book serves as a method to do just that. This process we are going on together is a journey of intimacy with God, understanding your **mandate, messages, and methods**, and recognizing the **grace** that runs through all three. It's about recognizing that your identity is not what you're simply good at, but what you are **graced** for.

Education can enhance your skills, but **grace empowers** you to fulfill your God-given purpose. Understanding your grace allows you to see the divine connections God places in your life, guiding you to align with His purpose.

If you're hiding your gifts, unsure of your true kingdom identity, or retreating from visibility, it's time to do more identity work—with God's grace at the center.

Identity work isn't something you engage in one time for clarity—it's an ongoing journey of discovery and growth. First, it's about building that personal relationship with God, experiencing Him in your life, and continually deepening that connection. Then, it's about turning that inward gaze and getting to know yourself better—your strengths, your weaknesses, your passions.

But it doesn't stop there. It's also about understanding God's purpose for you here on earth—your **mandate**, the **messages** you're meant to share, the **assignments** you're called to fulfill. And let's not forget about the how—the **methods,** the **strategies,** the **wisdom,** the **grace** that God provides to help you along the way.

So, in a nutshell, identity work is about knowing God intimately, understanding yourself as revealed by God, and discerning your divine calling and how to live it out authentically. And at every step of that journey—from knowing God, to knowing yourself, to walking out your assignment—it is **His empowering grace that makes it all possible.**

Contents

Part 1

Getting To Know Your Identity Pathway

Chapter 1

Kingdom Identity

"Take the word of God to your soul until you identify who you are." Apostle JB Makananisa

Your kingdom identity is not something you invent; it is something God reveals and sustains by His grace. It is the way He has woven you into the fabric of His Kingdom—a unique thread designed to carry His presence, His authority, and His assignment in the earth. To understand kingdom identity is to understand who God is, who you are in Him, what He has sent you to do, and how His grace empowers you to do it.

The Kingdom of God is vast, extending beyond the boundaries of any institution or tradition. And your identity, rooted in His Kingdom, is equally boundless. Your kingdom identity is more than a title or a role; it's understanding a mandate from God—*your* mandate—that reveals why you were sent to this earth. This concept transcends traditional career paths and societal roles, emphasizing a deeper, spiritual calling: a vocation. It's about understanding who God is, who you are, what He wants you to do, and how His grace enables you to do it.

Your kingdom identity is not about fitting into a predefined mold but embracing the unique role and calling God has placed on your life. It's about recognizing that your identity is intricately woven into the fabric of His Kingdom, where every aspect of who you are finds its fullest expression.

The word of God will reveal who you really are. It is through grace that you are both formed and empowered to fulfill your mandate. It wasn't until I began to understand the importance of this reality that I began to understand my true identity. **I realized that my worth was not defined by my achievements or titles but by the grace and gifts God had bestowed upon me.** Grace is a crucial component of kingdom identity. It is through grace that you are empowered to fulfill your mandate. Grace is not something you earn through education or achievement; it is a gift from God that enables you to do what you could never do on your own.

For example, I initially struggled with the idea of building a business and nonprofit based on something I wasn't naturally skilled at. However, God showed me that it's not about what I'm good at—it's about what I'm graced for. This understanding of my mandate, my vocation, allowed me to rely on God's strength and wisdom rather than my own abilities.

Building a habit of intimacy with God is essential for uncovering your true kingdom identity. This involves regular prayer, reflection, and listening for God's voice. It also means being open to the ways God speaks to you, whether through scripture, personal revelations, or the insights of those He places in your life.

Through the ups and downs of life, I've come to understand that embracing my kingdom identity is a journey—a continual process of seeking God, discovering more of myself, and aligning with His divine purpose. It's about stepping into the fullness of who God created me to be and living out His Kingdom purposes with grace and confidence.

As you journey through the pages of this book my hope is

that you'll discover the transformative power of kingdom identity in your own life. May you embrace the vastness of who you are in God's Kingdom and step boldly into the unique calling He has placed on your life, trusting that His grace is enough to carry you there.

The Power of Knowing Your Kingdom Mandate

Brand With Grace was created with the focus of your *vocation*, your *mandate*, bestowed upon you by God, throughout every process of the pathway. From the very beginning of this journey you will ask the Holy Spirit to reveal why you were sent. This journey is strategic, starting with hearing God and responding to His call. It's about creating an atmosphere that allows you to align with the Father and to live out, to release what He has created you to do.

God's mandate for his people is not a new concept. You can find the first mention of *mandate*—God's instruction, His decree, His *command*—given in the Bible. In Genesis 1:26-28, we read where God gives the first humans, Adam and Eve, their mandate, their vocation: to be fruitful, multiply, and subdue the earth. This passage of scripture is sometimes called the Creation Mandate, one that extends to all Christians, calling us to live with God-given purpose and authority.

When I first realized I had never asked God about my personal mandate, I sought Him for direction and felt the weight of His response. He told me my mandate was to restore originality and creativity to the body of believers, particularly in the marketplace. At first, I doubted this calling, feeling unworthy and overwhelmed. However, as I spent more time with God, He revealed the significance of this mandate not just for me, but for all believers. Understanding your mandate opens up so much for you, guiding your actions and decisions.

Just as we saw with Abraham, Isaac, and Solomon, mandate never stands alone. God does not hand you a heavenly assignment and then leave you to figure it out in your own strength. Mandate always comes wrapped in grace and backed by authority. When God reveals why He sent you and what He has called you to restore, He also releases the grace you need to walk it out and the authority you need to carry it. Your Kingdom mandate is not just a description of your calling; it is a doorway into God's empowering presence, His provision, and His backing for the work He has entrusted to you.

Knowing your mandate brings a big AHA! moment. It allows you to understand God's calling for your life and gives you the confidence to pursue it. My personal mandate, to restore originality and creativity to the body of believers, extends beyond business into all areas of my life. It's about creating an environment where others can seek God and discover their own mandates.

A *mandate* is different from a *purpose*. While purpose is about the intended use or goal of something, a mandate is a divine order that comes with authority. Only mankind can have a mandate, and with it comes the authority to act in a certain way, as given by God. This authority is crucial because it empowers you to fulfill your divine assignments.

When you operate within your mandate, you do so with the authority and provision from God. This ensures that you have everything you need to reach your destiny. Unlike purpose, which can be completed and leave you searching for the next thing, a mandate continually drives you toward your ultimate goal, keeping you aligned with God's plan.

Understanding your mandate allows you to navigate life's challenges with clarity and confidence. It helps you know what to say **yes** or **no** to and ensures you are operating within the authority God has given you. This understanding transforms your approach to life and business, making every action intentional and aligned with your divine calling.

Through the process that I will share in this book, I've seen people from all walks of life discover their mandates and transform their lives. Whether you're a business owner, a creative, in ministry, or a professional, understanding your mandate empowers you to walk in your unique calling with confidence and authority.

Your mandate is a beacon, a guiding star that illuminates your path and empowers you to make a lasting impact. It's an invitation to step into your divine assignment with confidence and boldness, knowing that you are equipped and authorized to fulfill it.

Understanding your mandate is not a destination but a continual journey of discovery and growth. Your mandate from God is continuous and layered. It's about consistently seeking God's guidance, being open to His direction, and walking in the authority He has given you. As you move forward, may you be inspired to live out your mandate fully, bringing originality and creativity into every sphere of your influence.

Let this book be a starting point—a catalyst for deeper exploration and a more profound connection with your divine calling. Embrace your mandate, walk in your authority, and transform your world. The journey has only just begun.

The Identity Pathway: Brand with Grace

God said to me, *People are branding what they want to become and not what I called them to be.* From this encounter, the Holy Spirit began to instruct me about how to bring solutions and awareness to what was on His heart. **Brand with Grace** was birthed as a journal, an experience, and is now a book. It's the solution to *not* conforming to an identity contrary to the one God called you to have and *not* building what God did not instruct you to build.

Think of branding with the grace of God as being yielded to His Spirit. You're yielded to whatever He wants you to do with whatever it is He's called you to create, build, or steward on the earth. Also, when I speak about a brand, I'm not just speaking about a personal brand. Your brand could be your business, service, or program. It could be something new or another leg or tier of what God is calling you to create or steward.

I'm convinced that for you to move boldly in your assignments here on earth, you need to understand the grace you carry. Understanding the grace you carry—and how to walk in it—begins to happen when you focus on knowing God and understanding your identity. This empowering grace works regardless of your skill, education, family status, or how many times you read the Bible all the way through.

This pattern of continuously seeking God and progressively growing in understanding our identity and the grace we carry is the heart of *Brand with Grace*. It's what I call the *identity pathway.* You should never get tired of re-engaging with God and sitting at His feet. You spend time with God not because you need anything from Him, but because you want to know Him more intimately.

At the foundation of *Brand with Grace* is the goal of growing in intimacy with and knowledge of God—and, in turn, knowing yourself. Through the pages of this book, you will find an *invitation*. If you accept it, this invitation is designed to help you dig deeper into the messages and ultimately encounter God in new ways. This entire experience should naturally immerse you in your identity with God. However, before we delve into identity, we need to begin by re-engaging with God through *Encounter* and *Communion*. A key component of encountering and communing with God is to continuously seek Him. Let's start by exploring what it takes to develop a practice or habit of continuously seeking God.

Becoming a Continuous Seeker of God

This book and companion journal will guide you through the identity pathway, a continuous, evolving process of seeking and understanding your true kingdom identity. The goal is to provide you with the tools and insights to make identity work a habitual practice, fostering a deeper relationship with God and a clearer understanding of your role within His Kingdom.

At the heart of the identity pathway is the intentionality of seeking God. This practice runs through all the invitations you get to accept at the end of each section—seeking God and growing in intimacy with Him. Before I share in detail the specific journey that is along this pathway, I want you to delve into the barriers that can prevent you from seeking God and ultimately making progress toward understanding your true kingdom identity.

1. The Myth of Self-Made Identity

From childhood, you may have been taught that you could be whoever you wanted to be. This mindset, though well-intentioned, is a barrier to seeking God. It ingrains in you a false sense of control over your destiny. You must shift your mindset to understand that you can only be who God designed you to be. When you believe you are the author of your destiny, you disregard the need to seek God's mind and will for your life. Seeking God continuously is not a one-time event, but a lifestyle.

2. The Illusion of Qualification

Another barrier is the belief that education, certification, degrees, and training validate or make you successful. You can unconsciously pursue these qualifications thinking they grant you authority, but true authority comes from seeking God. These worldly qualifications can become idols, causing you to rely more on your achievements than on God's wisdom and guidance. It's time to recognize that your true value and identity come from God, not from your accomplishments.

3. The Misplaced Starting Point

In life, but more prevalent in business, many start with *Why* instead of *Who*. As believers, while understanding your *Why* is important, it should not precede understanding your *Who*. Starting with *Who* sets the right foundation. It aligns our hearts with God's heart, ensuring that our actions are in harmony with His will. As we walk in the truth of who we are in Christ, we become vessels through which His light shines brightly in the world, impacting not only our businesses but also the lives of those around us.

Your foundation should be your identity in Christ, and this understanding comes from seeking God. When you seek God, you gain revelation about who you are in Him. This revelation transforms your approach to business and every other sphere of your life.

Breaking the Barriers

To move past these barriers, you need to adopt a continuous, heartfelt pursuit of God:

- Repentance: Start by repenting for the times you have substituted God's wisdom with your own. Acknowledge your need for Him and ask Him to reveal His heart to you.

- Agreement with God: Come into agreement with who God says you are. Believe in His promises and align yourself with His will.

- Spending time with God: Make seeking God a daily habit. Use tools like the *Brand with Grace Journal* to guide your conversations with Him and deepen your understanding of your kingdom identity.

Empowering Grace Through Seeking God

When you seek God, you gain access to His mind, His information, His revelation, and His connection. This empowers you to operate in your true identity and fulfill your divine calling in life and business. You are no longer just trying to pass the test or obtain qualifications; you are engaging with God to receive continuous guidance and revelation. And as you do, His grace begins to shape how you think, how you see yourself, and how you show up in every area of your life.

Let's make a commitment today: *I will seek God*. This commitment is not just for today but for every day moving forward. Matthew 6:33 NKJV reminds us to "seek first the kingdom of God and His righteousness, and all these things shall be added to you." This verse is not just a good saying; it is a principle that should manifest in your life and businesses. As you seek God, you will see His tangible presence as His blessings chase you down.

Practical Steps to Seek God

- Use the *Brand with Grace Journal*: Start with the daily spiritual exercise sections. Spend time journaling with the Father, Son, and Holy Spirit and let their presence wash over you.

- Meditate on what you sense God is saying: Reflect on the revelations God gives you and allow them to transform your heart and mind.

- Pray continuously: Engage in continuous communication with God. Ask Him questions and patiently and confidently wait for the answers. Build a habit of seeking His guidance in every aspect of your life and business.

Prayer for Seeking God

Father God, thank You. I pray for Your grace, Your anointing, and Your wisdom to flow in my life, work, and businesses. Help me to seek You continuously and to repent for the times I have relied on my own understanding. I come into agreement with who You say I am and commit to seeking You above all else. Let Matthew 6:33 manifest in my life as I pursue Your kingdom and Your righteousness. In Jesus' name. Amen.

Part 2

Navigating The Identity Pathway

Chapter 2

Hearing God

As you begin to navigate the identity pathway, it is important for you to understand that you have the ability to hear from the Holy Spirit. If you heard from Him once, you can hear from Him again. Because if God heard *you* once—when you received Him as your Savior—He still hears you. The same grace that saved you also opens your spiritual ears and invites you into ongoing conversation with Him. This ability to hear God is not something you earn; it is part of His grace toward you.

Sometimes we get distracted or try to hear from God through our natural ears. But it's important to remember that God is a *Spirit*. So when He speaks to us, we hear Him through our *spiritual* ears, as well as our other senses; God can speak to us through visions, dreams, smells—and in other ways He chooses to communicate.

You don't have to earn the ability to hear God's voice; He's always speaking, and He speaks to you. He wants to reveal Himself, and He wants to communicate with you.

So if you haven't already, begin by making this simple declaration right now: *I have the ability to hear from God.*

Typically, we go to the Lord to speak to Him in prayer; but that is often just us speaking *to* Him. We need to also go to Him expecting Him to talk back. There should be a dialogue happening, not just a monologue.

God can also speak to us when we don't expect it or want Him to. For example, if we are moving forward on a plan or goal and then we feel God's conviction and a "STOP!" we know we are hearing from God and that He is directing us at that moment.

God gives us a command to seek Him because He desires to commune with us. The more we seek, the more we hear and the greater our confidence becomes. *But seek first the kingdom of God and His righteousness, and all these things shall be added to you* (Matthew 6:33 NKJV).

Your confidence in your ability to hear God is vital to every aspect of your life—because your ability to hear God enables you to make wise decisions. It helps you to operate from a place of wisdom when the Holy Spirit is present with you, guiding you and giving you new and creative ideas.

God doesn't want to hold anything back from you. He wants you to know who you are, how He's called you to serve, what He's moving you to, where you have the most influence, and how He's advocating for you. And that's how you can move in holy boldness and confidence—because you're doing what God called you to do. When you are in that flow with Him, He is going to make sure that you are operating in excellence and give you strategies needed for what He's called you to do. When you know you can hear from Him, you will receive those strategies.

However, when you *don't* realize that you can hear from God to get those strategies, when you don't realize that the veil is torn and you can go to the Father for what you need, then you begin to buy into programs that aren't necessary for you. You can spend a lot of time and money trying to decide what it is that you're called to do—when it is not a secret and shouldn't be that hard to figure out.

God wants you to know who you are, and nobody (unless truly led by God to do so) can tell you exactly who that is. God is waiting and willing to reveal to you who He created you to be.

It's also important to remember that when God speaks to you, it will always come from a place of peace and love. You can recognize that it is His voice because He speaks from the inside and will tug on your heart.

An Experience with Hearing God

I want to share a personal story about hearing God so you can understand how He will speak quietly as an inner voice, often when you least expect it. This happened a few years ago when I began to discern what God was calling me to do.

At the time, I was homeschooling my three children and decided to take them on a walk. During that walk, I heard that small voice of the Holy Spirit give me a formula—*ROO>ROI—ROO is greater than ROI*. It kind of caught me off-guard a little (since I was just walking and not expecting to hear from the Lord at the time), but I responded in my heart and asked the Lord what ROO meant, and He said, "R*eturn on Obedience*."

I recognized it as the voice of the Holy Spirit, because He was teaching me something new. I had never heard the phrase *Return on Obedience* or *ROO*, so I knew it was the Lord sharing wisdom with me. Over time I have learned that God was showing me a formula for living in obedience with Him and understanding how God multiplies in our lives. He was inviting me to live out this formula and be an example of what obedience to God brings.

This personal story shows how God will give you the information you need so you are able to do the work He has called you to do. And it's all based on your ability to realize that you **can** hear from God.

Once you understand that you **do** hear from God, you will begin to experience Him through all of your senses. You'll be able to hear Him when you're awake and have dreams when you're asleep. You'll also begin to receive answers from Him to questions you have asked before that you've never been able to answer.

Back in the Garden of Eden, Satan deceived Adam and Eve with the first lie, telling them that God didn't really mean what He told them. The enemy will still try to convince you of that today. But if you have confidence in the fact that you hear from the Lord, he won't be able to trick you.

It is your birthright to know that God speaks to you. You have the ability to cancel the enemy's lies and move swiftly with rapid obedience, like the Psalmist mentions in Psalm 119:60 (NLT): *I will hurry, without delay, to obey your commands.*

You can also move with radical obedience because you know who you are, you know what you are called to, you know where your identity is, and you know what you've been influenced to do. You can begin to operate confidently in those situations where God has empowered you.

Invitation

*Decree this aloud, **I hear God!***

Prayer

Father, I thank You so much that I can be assured that I hear from You. As I take the time to sit with this book, I pray that my eyes will become open, my ears will become open, and I will begin to dream dreams and see visions. God, as prophesied by Your prophet Joel in the Bible, I believe this is a season where You are pouring out more of Your Spirit. I'm coming to a place where I can confidently say that I hear from You and am directed by You. You're giving me original strategies to operate in my business, in my life, in my family, and with my children. I bless You, God, for giving me the ability to speak life into anyone who will listen. I thank You for the ability that You have given me to sharpen others. I thank You for helping me dream again, hear Your voice, move in confidence, and understand that I have original strategies and blueprints for everything that You're calling me into.

God, I pray Your Spirit will cover me. I pray for an internal peace that no man and no demon can penetrate, Father, in the name of Jesus. Amen.

Discerning God

Now that you are aware of your ability to hear God (as your birthright), the next step along the identity pathway is to learn and/or practice how to *discern* the voice of God.

Discerning God in the Bible

Meanwhile, the boy Samuel served the Lord by assisting Eli. Now in those days, messages from the Lord were very rare, and visions were quite uncommon. One night Eli, who was almost blind by now, had gone to bed. The lamp of God had not yet gone out, and Samuel was sleeping in the Tabernacle near the Ark of God. Suddenly the Lord called out, "Samuel!" "Yes?" Samuel replied. "What is it?" (1 Samuel 3:1-4 NLT)

Notice there was not a struggle for Samuel to hear God speaking even though the Scriptures tell us that during that time, it was rare for God to speak and visions were uncommon. Yet, Samuel could hear God. He could hear a voice. He just couldn't discern from whom it came.

To summarize what happened: Samuel gets up out of bed and says to Eli, *Here I am. Did you call me?* And Eli replies, *I didn't call you, go back to bed.* So he did. Then the Lord called out again, *Samuel!*

What was the Lord doing? He was waiting for a response. He was waiting for Samuel to discern His voice, just like I believe He's doing with some of us now.

So he said to Samuel, "Go and lie down again, and if someone calls again, say, 'Speak, Lord, your servant is listening.'" So Samuel went back to bed. And the Lord came and called as before, "Samuel! Samuel!" And Samuel replied, "Speak, your servant is listening." Then the Lord said to Samuel, "I am about to do a shocking thing in Israel. I am going to carry out all my threats against Eli and his family, from beginning to end. I have warned him that judgment is coming upon his family forever because his sons are blaspheming God and he hasn't disciplined them. So I have vowed that the sins of Eli and his sons will never be forgiven by sacrifices or offerings." (1 Samuel 3:9-14 NLT)

God began to speak to Samuel about Eli, and as He did this,

He began to reveal his destiny; it was important that he was able to discern God's voice, because this was the beginning of his calling as a prophet. He could hear God speak, but he did not discern the voice of the Lord until Eli explained it to him. Not only is it important for you to be able to discern God's audible voice, but to also discern Him through your senses.

Taste and see that the Lord is good. Oh the joys of those who take refuge in Him. (Psalm 34:8 NLT)

Discerning how God speaks is recognizing that it *is* God speaking, and He not only speaks audibly but also through your senses. And just like Samuel, as you begin to understand how God speaks to you, you can begin to be used by Him in greater measure.

Discernment is how you will know your next assignment: by revelation and the inspired Word of God. In fact, in the scriptures, there are many examples of divine encounters that have allowed great men and women to recognize their God given destinies.

The Lord had said to Abram, "Leave your native country, your relatives, and your father's family, and go to the land that I will show you. I will make you into a great nation. I will bless you and make you famous, and you will be a blessing to others. I will bless those who bless you and curse those who treat you with contempt. All the families on earth will be blessed through you." So Abram departed as the Lord had instructed, and Lot went with him. Abram was seventy-five years old when he left Haran. (Genesis 12:1-4 MSG)

There was no specific formula that Abram had to follow to

hear God. He discerned the voice of the Lord and he obeyed. As you continue to read through this passage from Genesis 12, you will begin to realize that Abram didn't even know where he was going. He followed the Lord's instructions—not knowing where He was leading him—because he discerned that God was speaking to him and he obeyed. And remember, this is before the veil was even torn, which speaks immeasurably about God still being the same God. He wants to and does speak; you just have to be able to discern His voice.

Now, let's take a look at another example from the New Testament.

> As I was on the road, approaching Damascus about noon, a very bright light from heaven suddenly shone down around me. I fell to the ground and heard a voice saying to me, "Saul, Saul, why are you persecuting me?" "Who are you, Lord?" I asked. And the voice replied, "I am Jesus the Nazarene, the one you are persecuting." (Acts 22:6-8 NLT)

Saul (who will later become Paul) was persecuting Christians. He did not have a relationship with God, but he still heard a voice. It was a question that he could hear, even though he couldn't discern who was speaking. But when God speaks, there is authority behind it. Even when God is speaking through dreams or perception or your senses, there is still an authority there. It is something you can't duplicate.

Sometimes, for me, it feels like a burning in my heart, an intense connection. The feeling commands my attention; I just sense it's Someone of authority.

As we examine the scriptures, that strong sense of connection is what we see with Saul. Even though he didn't know who he was speaking to, he still answered, *Who are you, my*

Lord? because he connected with the authority in the voice.

> "'Who are you, lord?" I asked. And the voice replied, "I am Jesus the Nazarene, the one you are persecuting." The people with me saw the light but didn't understand the voice speaking to me. I asked, "What should I do, Lord?" And the Lord told me, "Get up and go into Damascus, and there you will be told everything you are to do." (Act 22: 8-10 NLT)

Did you catch that? Destiny comes through revelation from the Father. This is why it's so important to spend time learning how to hear from and respond to God.

Because the key to getting to the next step in your destiny, even before you uncover the identity and message, is to understand that you must have encounters with your Heavenly Father. It doesn't have to be a sensational encounter, it's just God speaking to you.

I want you to consider: When was the last time you met with Jesus—more specifically, had an encounter with your Heavenly Father? It could include something He said or something He showed you. Sometimes He may do something like put a flower, soft rays of sunlight through trees, or a doe and her fawn in your path as you pray during your morning walk; these are gifts from the Lord, and He uses them to gently speak to your soul. It does not have to be a colossal, monumental, overwhelming type experience—you'll know when God is speaking to you. And as you develop that awareness, you'll begin to understand more of what God is saying. But you *do* have to practice this, and there are exercises you can do to hear and discern the voice of the Lord; because it is important as you do life and business with God as a believer that you encounter Him.

Sometimes I'll ask God, *Where are You today? What's on Your heart today?* I don't have to stop what I'm doing because I realize that God is a Spirit and speaks to me internally, so I can go about my day and hear God speak back. It's a beautiful thing—but it happens through relationship and intention.

Repetition and familiarity also help to discern how God speaks. For instance, I have dreams almost every night, and God often speaks to me through them. When He shows me in a vision or a dream that a particular incident is happening in my house, I discern—through prayer—whether it is truly going to happen or if it's something in which I need to quickly act upon. I have found by repetition that when the scene or location of a dream happens in my home, I must pay attention to what God may be revealing.

That's how He speaks to me; that's how I've built my language with God and how He typically responds to me. Your way may be different, and that's okay.

Sometimes He will use familiar—and often daily—places, people, or symbols to communicate. As you spend time with and stay attentive to God, you begin to develop your language with Him and learn to discern His voice.

The important thing to remember is that God is going to continue to unlock what He wants you to do in your assignment with Him. Just like He did with (Saul) Paul in the Bible.

> I was blinded by the intense light and had to be led by the hand to Damascus by my companions. A man named Ananias lived there. He was a godly man, deeply devoted to the law, and well regarded by all the Jews of Damascus. He came and stood beside me and said, "Brother Saul, regain your sight." And that very moment I could see him!

Then he told me, "The God of our ancestors has chosen you to know his will and to see the Righteous One and hear him speak." (Acts 22:11-14 NLT)

That is my prayer for you. I believe that the God of our ancestors has destined **you** to know His plan for your life and business, to see the Holy One and to hear His voice.

For you are to be his witness, telling everyone what you have seen and heard. What are you waiting for? Get up and be baptized. Have your sins washed away by calling on the name of the Lord. (Acts 22:15-16 NLT)

This is so significant, because as I was creating this pathway, the Lord spoke to me and said, *You are Ananias and you are helping Ananiases, and what you are releasing is going to help others to see what it is that they're supposed to do.* My response was "Okay, God." And then, the very next day, God sent confirmation of that same word through a phone call I had with a complete stranger. That word was not just a nice metaphor; it was a picture of grace. Just as God graced Ananias to help Paul see and step into his assignment, God was showing me the grace on my life to help others see and step into theirs. Your ability to help others in their identity and destiny is always tied to the specific grace God has given you.

As you're reading this right now you may be unsure of what your next step is. Or maybe you've heard things that go against what feels right as you walk through building out your brand and your identity with God and how to reveal it to the people you're called to serve. I believe that God is going to give you some amazing encounters by revelation as you continue to journey on and engage the Holy Spirit with the work you're going to do and the invitations you're going to accept. He's going to unlock some things for you that you have been

Chapter 3

Responding to God

How do you respond to God? Do you respond to God?

Although you, as a believer, should have a reverent fear of the Lord, sometimes you can find yourself in a state of near paralysis when it comes to responding to God. That's why we need not only reverence, but also a revelation of His grace and His heart toward us.

This was the case for me when the Holy Spirit gave me a revelation one day a couple of years ago. At the time, I was hearing from the Lord and was doing well by responding with my actions. But what I didn't realize was that I had been receiving directions from God and then acting on them without stopping to converse with Him about them first.

I wasn't responding (in words) at all! And the Holy Spirit revealed to me that the reason behind my behavior was the relationship I had with God. At the time, I had a view of Him that was almost like that of a military commander. I had a healthy fear of Him, but I was almost taking it too far and seeing God only as my commander, with me as His servant—there was no Father/child or friendship in our relationship.

Responding to God is tied to your relationship with Him and how you see what He reveals to you about Himself. He is, in fact, our Lord and our Savior. He is *El Shaddai*, the covering over our heads. But He is also our friend and our Father.

When you only see Him as a distant commander, responding can feel like pressure and performance. But when you see Him as Father and friend, you begin to respond from a place of love and grace, not fear and performance.

And the amazing thing is, if you struggle with seeing Him this way (often because of issues with your father in the natural world), you can ask Him to teach you. He will hold your hand and walk you through it, step by step.

In my own situation, I just opened up to Him and confessed how I had been putting limits on our relationship; and I recognized how it was affecting my responses to Him— but I wanted Him to help me change.

If this sounds like you, He wants you to do the same. He wants to come in close with you. He wants you to camp out with Him, experience Him and have a back-and-forth dialogue—but you have to choose to respond to Him.

Responding in the Bible

An amazing Biblical example of responding to God and walking in relationship with Him is that of (Abram) Abraham.

> The Lord had said to Abram, "Leave your native country, your relatives, and your father's family, and go to the land that I will show you. I will make you into a great nation. I will bless you and make you famous, and you will be a blessing to others. I will bless those who bless you and curse those who treat you with contempt. All the families on earth will be blessed through you." So Abram departed as the Lord had instructed, and Lot went with him. Abram was seventy-five years old when he left Haran. (Genesis 12:1-4 NLT)

When you look at this passage of Scripture, you see that Abram isn't asking God, "Why am I doing this? Where am I going? Can I take Lot?" He just responds by doing what God said.

> Then the Lord appeared to Abram and said, "I will give this land to your descendants." And Abram built an altar there and dedicated it to the Lord, who had appeared to him. (Genesis 12:7 NLT)

Unlike the first encounter, in this second one, Abram does interact with the Lord by building an altar. Even though it does not tell us what he said, we see that Abram responded because of his relationship with God.

> After Lot separated from him, Yahweh spoke to Abram. "Lift up your eyes and look around you to the north, the south, the east, and the west, as far as you can see in every direction is the land I will give to you forever, to you and your seed. I will multiply them until they are as numerous as the specks of dust on the earth. If anyone could count the dust of the earth, then your offspring could also be counted. Now get up and walk through the land, its length, and its breadth. All the land you walk upon will be my gift to you." Abram moved his camp and settled by the oaks of Mamre, which are at Hebron, and there he built an altar to the Lord. (Genesis 13:14-18 TPT; ESV)

Again, although we don't see Abram speaking verbally to God, he responds by his obedience to follow His directions. And as we continue to follow his journey with the Lord, we see that the more he opens up to Him, the more God speaks to him. And vice versa.

> Some time later, the Lord spoke to Abram in a vision and said to him, "Do not be afraid, Abram, for I will protect you, and your reward will be great." But Abram replied, "O Sovereign Lord, what good are all your blessings when I don't

even have a son? Since you've given me no children, Eliezer of Damascus, a servant in my household, will inherit all my wealth. You have given me no descendants of my own, so one of my servants will be my heir." (Genesis 15:1-3 NLT)

Now we see Abram responding to God verbally about what He's been saying to him. Because by this point, he is probably wondering when this promise—this seed, these descendants the Lord's been talking about—is ever going to show up! So he responds to God and asks Him about it.

God answers Abram: *Then the Lord said to him, "No, your servant will not be your heir, for you will have a son of your own who will be your heir* (Genesis 15:4 NLT). We now see an intimate relationship forming between Abram and the Lord as they respond and dialogue with one another.

Abram is no longer just responding by his obedience but now has a relationship with God where he is responding to Him. And this is a perfect picture for us to remember.

God wants you to respond to Him. He wants you to inquire of Him. He wants you to inquire about His promises. You don't have to wait for Him to show up and talk to you; you can reach out to Him and He will show up. As we see with Abram, God will continue to show up, both to remind you of what He said and to encourage you.

Another example from scripture is in 1 Samuel. God called Samuel when he was serving Eli. He answered, but he answered the wrong person. He thought it was Eli who was calling him, so he responded to him several times. But then, in verses 7-11, we see this:

Then Eli realized it was the LORD who was calling the boy. So he said to Samuel, "Go and lie down again, and if someone calls again, say, 'Speak, LORD, your servant is listening.'" So Samuel went back to bed. And the LORD came and called as before, "Samuel! Samuel!" And Samuel replied, "Speak, your servant is listening." Then the LORD said to Samuel, "I am about to do a shocking thing in Israel." (1 Samuel 3:7-11 NLT)

It's interesting to note that God could have just started talking to Samuel. But instead, He waited until Samuel responded and acknowledged it was the Lord speaking to him before He started talking to him. Which again, just shows how important it is to respond to God.

The story of Moses and the burning bush in Exodus 3 also demonstrates an intimate relationship with the Lord that encourages a response:

One day Moses was tending the flock of his father-in-law, Jethro, the priest of Midian. He led the flock far into the wilderness and came to Sinai, the mountain of God. There the angel of the LORD appeared to him in a blazing fire from the middle of a bush. Moses stared in amazement.

Though the bush was engulfed in flames, it didn't burn up. "This is amazing," Moses said to himself. "Why isn't that bush burning up? I must go see it." When the LORD saw Moses coming to take a closer look, God called to him from the middle of the bush, "Moses! Moses!" "Here I am!" Moses replied. (Exodus 3:1-4 NLT)

Again, we see another example of how God could've just called to Moses and began to speak to him. But instead, He waited until Moses responded by drawing closer and inquiring of Him first. Moses said, "I must go see it." And that's how we should be with things of the Lord. God wants us to be hungry and thirsty for what He's showing us. He wants us to turn to Him and inquire, to ask Where are You in this, God?

And when Moses inquired, God responded:

> "Do not come any closer," the LORD warned. "Take off your sandals, for you are standing on holy ground. I am the God of your father—the God of Abraham, the God of Issac, and the God of Jacob." (Exodus 3:5, 6a NLT)

The Old Testament isn't the only place we find examples of this two-way communication between God and His people. We also see it in the New Testament with Saul in Acts 22 as he describes his experience on the road to Damascus.

> I fell to the ground and heard a voice saying to me, "Saul, Saul, why are you persecuting me?" "Who are you, Lord?" I asked. And the voice replied, "I am Jesus the Nazarene, the one you are persecuting." The people with me saw the light but didn't understand the voice speaking to me. I asked, "What should I do, Lord?" And the Lord told me, "Get up and go into Damascus, and there you will be told everything you are to do." (Acts 22:7-10 NLT)

Again, we see the Lord speaking to (Saul) Paul and he responds. And when he does, the Lord gives him specific instructions about what he is to do next.

Meditation Verse

Hear me as I pray, O LORD. Be merciful and answer me! My heart has heard you say, "Come and talk with me." And my heart responds, "LORD, I am coming." (Psalm 27:7-8 NLT)

Responding to the Lord is important, because thanks to

Jesus, you have access to God. The veil is torn. God is inviting you in. You no longer have to kill the goat or the turtledove before you're able to go before your Father, your Daddy, your Lord. You can and should respond to God because He is waiting for you. He's waiting to answer you. He's waiting for you to enter into a deeper level of intimacy with Him.

Invitation

Recall one or two things God has said to you about which you have not responded. Then, take some time to sit with the Lord and respond to Him specifically around those areas. Be sure to write down what He shares with you!

Prayer

Father God, You're amazing. Help me grow in my relationship with You. Help me know that I can respond to You in different ways. God, help me not be paralyzed by You being my Lord, governor, and ruler. Let me open up and let You into every area of my life and build a relationship with You as my Father and my friend.

God, I break every lie of the enemy—that I am not able to respond to You, that it's humility not to speak, that it's humility just to do and not to inquire. But I say, Speak, Lord God, I hear You. I desire You, and I am responding. I am responding in my spirit. I am responding by obedience to You, God. And I will respond in relationship to You."
God, I pray for peace and freedom for myself and pray that I will come to understand that You will begin to speak to me about things I did not inquire about years ago. God, I pray that

You would help me to walk into more of who I am, as I open up and begin to respond to You, in Jesus's name. Amen.

Chapter 4

Understanding Your Kingdom Identity by Grace

As a believer, you know that your identity is found in Christ. But one of the most important things you need to understand is that it's impossible to worship a God you do not know. If you don't understand who God is, if you haven't met Him and had a personal encounter with Him, then you won't be able to truly understand your identity and receive instructions from God about what He is calling you to do.

Identity in the Bible: Knowing God, Knowing Yourself

This exact issue was happening in the Bible, which we see with Paul speaking to the Church in Acts 17.

So Paul, standing before the council, addressed them as follows: "Men of Athens, I notice that you are very religious in every way, for as I was walking along I saw your many shrines. And one of your altars had this inscription on it: 'To an Unknown God.' This God, whom you worship without knowing, is the one I'm telling you about. He is the God who made the world and everything in it. Since he is Lord of heaven and earth, he doesn't live in man-made temples, and human hands can't serve his needs—for he has no needs. He himself gives life and breath to everything, and he satisfies every need. From one man he created all the nations throughout the whole earth. He decided beforehand when they should rise and fall, and he determined their boundaries. His purpose was for the nations to seek after God and perhaps feel their way toward him and find him—though he is not far from any one of us. For in him we live and move and exist. As some of your own poets have said, 'We are his offspring.' And since this is true, we shouldn't think of God as an idol designed by craftsmen from gold or silver or stone." (Acts 17:22-29 NLT)

Let's pay attention to what Paul is saying here about creation. He says from one man God created all the nations throughout the whole earth to seek after Him and find Him. Because our identity is found in Him.

And as Paul explains to the church, we need to understand who God is and what His plan is for mankind—which is for us to seek Him, find Him, and walk through the door He opens for us, so we can know who we truly are.

When you begin to understand who God is, then you understand who you are. When you have a revelation about who God is to you, then He will tell you who you are to Him. He will let you know how He designed you and what He's called you to do.

If you don't know the God you worship, you need to meet Him today. You must have a desire, as Paul revealed, to feel your way toward Him and find Him (Acts 17: 27b NLT). He's not far from you, so you can know more about the God you worship. And knowing more about Him will help you know more about yourself.

When Jesus came to the region of Caesarea Philippi, he asked his disciples, "Who do people say that the Son of Man is?" "Well," they replied, "Some say John the Baptist, some say Elijah, and others say Jeremiah or one of the other prophets." Then he asked them, "But who do you say I am?" Simon Peter answered, "You are the Messiah, the Son of the living God." Jesus replied, "You are blessed, Simon son of John, because my Father in heaven has revealed this to you. You did not learn this from any human being. Now I say to you that you are Peter (which means *rock*), and upon this rock, I will build my church, and all the powers of hell will not conquer it. And I will give you the keys of the Kingdom of Heaven. Whatever you forbid on earth will be forbidden in heaven, and whatever you permit on earth will be permitted in heaven." (Matthew 16:13-19 NLT)

In the passage you just read in Matthew, you see that Peter had a revelation about God. And when you have a revelation about the identity of the One you serve, you will learn that your identity is in Christ.

Grace and Your Kingdom Identity

When Peter received that revelation—*You are the Messiah, the Son of the living God*—Jesus did not just affirm Peter's answer. He immediately responded with Peter's identity and assignment:

You are blessed, Simon son of John, because my Father in heaven has revealed this to you. Now I say to you that you are Peter (which means rock), and upon this rock I will build my church. (Matthew 16:17–18 NLT)

Revelation of who God is unlocked revelation of who Peter was and what he was called to do. But there is something else happening in this moment that we often overlook: **grace.**

Peter wasn't promoted because he was the most disciplined or the most put-together. He was a fisherman with a history of speaking too quickly, and later, he would even deny Jesus. Yet Jesus still chose him, renamed him, and entrusted him with a foundational role in the Church.

What's the explanation for that? It is not self-effort. It is grace.

One of the most important truths you can learn about identity is this: **Grace doesn't just save you; grace shapes you.**

The apostle Paul puts it this way:

> But God's amazing grace has made me who I am, and his grace to me was not fruitless. In fact, I worked harder than all the rest, yet not in my own strength but God's, for his empowering grace is poured out upon me. (1 Corinthians 15:10 TPT)

Notice what Paul says first: *God's amazing grace has made me who I am.*

Your kingdom identity is not just your personality, your roles, or your background. Like Paul, you can say, "God's amazing grace has made me who I am."

Grace is God's active work in your life that forms, refines, and empowers who you are in Him.

A simple way the Holy Spirit taught me to understand is this: **Grace is God's ability.**

Grace is not just a concept; it is God's ability and sufficiency at work in you. Anywhere you feel weak, underqualified, or unsure of yourself, what you actually need is more of God's grace—more of His ability in that area.

Paul goes on to say: *This grace to me was not fruitless. In fact, I worked harder than all the rest, yet not in my own strength but God's.*

So grace does at least three things in the area of identity:

1. Grace defines who you are.
"God's amazing grace has made me who I am."

2. Grace makes your life fruitful.
"His grace to me was not fruitless."

3. Grace empowers your work.
"I worked, yet not in my own strength, but God's."

This is where kingdom identity and grace meet:

- God reveals who He is.

- In His presence, He reveals who you are.

- Then He empowers you by grace to walk out that identity and assignment.

Without grace, identity teaching becomes pressure: "Now that you know who you are, go make it happen."

With grace, identity becomes partnership: "Now that you know who you are, invite God's ability to move through you."

As you continue reading this chapter, keep this in mind:

You are not just discovering who you are; you are also discovering the specific grace God has placed on your life to fulfill your kingdom identity.

Invitation

Read Psalm 139 in three translations and take time to meditate on the words that God highlights for you.

Prayer

God, You're amazing. Help me to search for You as hidden treasure. Father, I am privileged that You are mindful of me and that You have created me and formed me into my unique identity. Thank You for always going before me and divinely connecting me. I pray that You would continue to open up my understanding and give me revelation into my spiritual identity. I bless You and thank You for everything that shall be revealed, In Jesus's name. Amen.

Identity, Grace, and Wealth

In my journey of creating the process and teachings in this book, I had another significant moment with the Lord. First, He revealed to me the importance of yielding to Him and seeking His guidance about who I am and what He has specifically called me to do. Through this revelation, I understood that success and wealth are intrinsically tied to understanding and walking in my true identity. Over time, He also began to show me that this connection between identity and wealth runs through someting else: **His grace**. I want to share this insight with you and hope you will see the connection between identity and wealth.

When I speak about wealth in the context of identity and God's purpose, it's crucial to distinguish between worldly wealth and the wealth that comes from God. Worldly wealth is usually defined by material possessions, financial abundance, and social status. It's measured by what you have accumulated, driven by self-interest and societal expectations. This type of wealth is fleeting, subject to the fluctuations of the economy, and disconnected from your true mandate.

This is where grace comes in: Godly wealth is about provision, abundance, and resources directly connected to your God-given identity and mandate. This wealth isn't about accumulating riches for personal gain but about having the necessary resources to fulfill God's purpose for your life. This provision includes, but is not limited to, financial resources. It encompasses ideas, strategies, innovations, solutions, tools, and relationships that God provides. This wealth is sustainable, fulfilling, and aligned with your spiritual and practical calling.

Godly wealth flows from a place of obedience and alignment with God's will. It is accessed through your relationship with Him as you grow in your understanding of who He is and who He has created you to be. As you walk in your true identity, God's empowering grace goes to work, opening doors and releasing the provision you need to carry out the work He has entrusted to you. Wealth and identity go hand-in-hand because this relationship naturally includes the provision and resources needed to carry out God's purposes for your life and business through the unique gifts and grace He has given you. Remember, wealth is not just financial gain but also ideas, tools, divine connections, and resources.

To walk into the provision God has provided for you, you must understand who you are. And as we've previously discussed, the only way to know who you are and what you're called to is through a relationship with Him. As you uncover who He is, He reveals to you who you are. Then, by His grace, He equips you for what He has called you to do. That is the beauty of growing in revelation through a relationship with the One who knows you best.

When you connect with your true kingdom identity, you can seek the heart of the Father and begin to walk in the ways of John 15:7 (NLT): *But if you remain in me and my words remain in you, you may ask for anything you want, and it will be granted!* You can go to the Father and ask Him according to His will, and He will give you what you ask for because you understand what to ask for. Your requests come into alignment with your identity and the grace on your life, and Heaven's provision follows that alighment.

God has placed you here on earth with access to everything that you will need to fulfill your destiny. Your understanding of your identity helps you grow in the faith needed to gain access to the resources, provisions and spiritual blessings that are available. Therefore, wealth isn't connected to righteousness only, but to identity. You don't have access to wealth because you are righteous; you have access to wealth because it's part of your assignment, part of how God is guiding you and shaping you. Since God is your Father, you stand under the umbrella of His provision when you are in His will. And it is His grace—His ability working in and through you—that connects your obedience to the resources prepared for your assignment.

Let's look at the life of Abraham and a few others to see the connection between identity and wealth through their stories.

Abraham: Wealth Through Covenant and Grace

Abraham's story in Genesis serves as a foundational example of how wealth is tied to identity. God's covenant with Abraham was clear:

The Lord had said to Abram, "Leave your native country, your relatives, and your father's family, and go to the land that I will show you. I will make you into a great nation. I will bless you and make you famous, and you will be a blessing to others. I will bless those who bless you and curse those who treat you with contempt. All the families on earth will be blessed through you." (Genesis 12:1-3, NLT)

This covenant established Abraham's identity as the father of a great nation and set the stage for his wealth. Genesis 13:2 (NLT) states, *Abram was very rich in livestock, silver, and gold.* This wealth resulted from his obedience to God's call and fulfilling his mandate. It was also the visible outworking of God's grace on his life—God's ability and favor backing the assignment he had been given.

Abraham's wealth was not for personal gain but to facilitate his role in God's plan. His identity as the father of a chosen people required resources to lead, protect, and provide for his family and followers. This abundance enabled him to bless others, aligning with the promise that *all the families on earth will be blessed through you.* In other words, Abraham's identity, grace, and wealth were all working together: his identity revealed his mandate, grace empowered him to walk it out, and wealth flowed as provision for that grace-filled assignment.

Isaac: Grace, Inheritance, and the Covenant Blessing

Isaac, Abraham's son, inherited not just wealth but the covenant blessing that accompanied his father's mission. Genesis 26:12-14 (NLT) illustrates this continuity:

When Isaac planted his crops that year, he harvested a hundred times more grain than he planted, for the Lord blessed him. He became a very rich man, and his wealth continued to grow. He acquired so many flocks of sheep and goats, herds of cattle, and servants that the Philistines became jealous of him.

Isaac's wealth manifested God's blessing, which was deeply tied to his identity as Abraham's son and the bearer of the covenant promise. The hundredfold harvest was not normal human ability; it was the grace of God—His supernatural sufficiency—in Isaac's everyday work. This abundance allowed Isaac to fulfill his role within God's overarching plan, further establishing the nation that God had promised to Abraham.

Solomon: Grace for Wisdom, Leadership, and Wealth

Solomon's story perfectly illustrates the connection between identity and wealth. When Solomon ascended to the throne, he asked God for wisdom to lead His people effectively. God's response was profound and multifaceted:

So God replied, "Because you have asked for wisdom in governing my people with justice and have not asked for a long life or wealth or the death of your enemies—I will give you what you asked for! I will give you a wise and understanding heart such as no one else has had or ever will have! And I will also give you what you did not ask for— riches and fame! No other king in all the world will be compared to you for the rest of your life!" (1 Kings 3:11-13, NLT)

Solomon's wealth was a divine provision granted because of his identity and his role as a wise and just ruler. This wealth was not merely for personal pleasure but to support his leadership and the construction of the temple, which was a central place of worship for Israel. God's gift of wisdom itself was a form of grace—His ability given to Solomon for leadership—and the riches and fame were grace-filled overflow attached to that identity and assignment.

The connection between identity and wealth, as seen in the lives of Abraham, Isaac, and Solomon, highlights a deep biblical truth: Wealth is a divine provision carried on the back of grace and tied to your covenant relationship with God and your identity. When you understand and embrace your true kingdom identity, you unlock the provision needed to fulfill your mandate and bless others. This principle encourages you to seek God's guidance, trust in His provision, and steward your resources for His glory and the advancement of His kingdom.

Invitation

Read all of Psalm 119 in its entirety. Meditate on your identity and the connection to wealth. How has your identity been tied to your wealth, and how do you see them being connected as you begin to accumulate greater levels of wealth and walk into greater levels of provision?

What level of provision are you believing God for based on what He's assigned you to do in this season?

Read Proverbs 8 in its entirety. In what areas of your life do you need to change so you can more reflect who God says you are?

Prayer

Father, I thank You for continuously revealing my identity and what You've called me to do in the earth. Thank You for Your provision that comes as I say "Yes" to You and seek Your wisdom to steward what You've given me. Hallelujah! I praise You for the wealth and provision You're releasing to me because I have access through my obedience and faithfulness. I honor and glorify You, in Christ Jesus's name. Amen.

Identity, Alignment, and Grace

There is one final piece that is also vitally important when it comes to understanding our identity, and that is alignment. And to better understand this component of your identity, we are going to look at Hezekiah in 2 Chronicles 29.

The backstory to King Hezekiah: There was a long line of kings before him who went back-and-forth between being righteous and following the ways of the Lord, or being wicked and perverting the temple. So when Hezekiah was 25 years old, he was named king and given the task of restoring the temple and changing the people's hearts back to God.

Basically, everything was out of alignment. The people were out of alignment. The temple was out of alignment. Everything was in a bad state. The people had turned their backs on the Lord and abandoned Him, and He was angry.

Hezekiah summoned the priests and the Levites to meet him at the temple and began to share with them what needed to be done.

My sons, do not neglect your duties any longer! The Lord has chosen you to stand in his presence, to minister to him, and to lead the people in worship and present offerings to him. (2 Chron. 29:11 NLT)

That is a holy king!

And that's all it took—for a righteous king to come in and say, "Look, this is what you're called to do. This is what you're supposed to be doing. I need you to get to work and do it." I don't know what they were doing before, but it wasn't aligned with their chosen calling. And right after Hezekiah spoke, the next verse tells us the Levites got right to work.

> These men called together their fellow Levites, and they all purified themselves. Then they began to cleanse the Temple of the Lord, just as the king had commanded. They were careful to follow all the Lord's instructions in their work. The priests went into the sanctuary of the Temple of the Lord to cleanse it, and they took out to the Temple courtyard all the defiled things they found. From there the Levites carted it all out to the Kidron Valley. They began the work in early spring, on the first day of the new year, and in eight days they had reached the entry room of the Lord's Temple. Then they purified the Temple of the Lord itself, which took another eight days. So the entire task was completed in sixteen days. (2 Chron. 29:15-17 NLT)

Throughout the chapter we see that the people went right to work and followed all the Lord's instructions, and the entire thing ended up being completed in 16 days. In fact, verses 35 and 36 say that the temple was restored to service and all the people rejoiced because of what God had done and how quickly everything had been accomplished.

That's the amazing power of identity and alignment, because once you know and understand who you are, you can operate in that identity. It's the power of God's amazing empowering grace that allows you to come under His umbrella of provision for whatever it is He has called you to do. And when everything works in alignment—your work, your life—can run smoothly.

The same is true for you as an individual. You need to be restored to your true identity and to serve in alignment with your God-given calling. Some of you may have gotten off track and are unsure of God's direction. You may have forgotten what God said to you or don't believe it to be true. Now, God is calling you back. He is a God of restoration—He restores you to Himself. He restores you to believe what He says about who you are and brings you back into alignment with His truth. When you operate within your calling and share what God has specifically given you the grace and authority to walk in, you align with your God-given gifts. You are then able to help others find their way toward their own gifts and callings.

You can't carry out your destiny without knowing your identity if you have no idea what direction to take. But when you know what you're called to do and you walk in it, you know what to say *yes* to and what to say *no* to. Your identity is what keeps you aligned and keeps you on track for everything God has called you to!

As you can see throughout this chapter, your kingdom identity is not something you manufacture; it is revealed as you know God, and it is sustained by His grace. Abraham, Isaac, Solomon, and Hezekiah each show us that identity, wealth, and alignment are not random—they flow from covenant relationship and from God's empowering ability at work in their lives. The same is true for you. As you uncover who God is and who He says you are, His grace shapes your identity, brings you into alignment, and releases the provision needed for your assignment. You were never meant to carry your calling in your own strength. Your identity is uncovered by grace, your wealth is stewarded by grace, and your alignment is maintained by grace, so that everything in your life points back to Him and advances His Kingdom.

Invitation

Read 2 Chronicles 29 in its entirety and reflect on how Hezekiah's understanding of his identity helped him not only to stay in alignment himself but to also help the people get back into alignment as well.

Prayer

God, You're amazing. I love You so much. I pray to go from revelation to revelation about who I am and what You call me to steward. Show me what is in my hands and how to use it with authority for Your glory. Help me stand in alignment and operate with a spirit of restoration. Restore anything in my life that is not in order. Help me hear, discern, and respond to Your voice as You give me instruction and lead me in what You have called me to do. I love and appreciate You so much.

And I thank You for this time, God, to read and meditate on Your restoration and how I have access to this restorative power through my identity. I appreciate You, Father, and love You so much—I'm in awe of You, oh Holy King. Thank You for choosing me. Thank You so much. In Jesus's name. Amen.

Chapter 5

Enemies of Identity

Now it's time to delve into what I call the "enemies of identity." These are tactical tools or weapons that the enemy uses, along with mindsets and behaviors we allow into our lives, which stagnate and block us from fully walking in our true kingdom identity.

We're going to examine four specific enemies: **competition, fear, lack of wisdom and revelation, and false humility.** This is not an exhaustive list, but these are the four I want to focus on.

As we explore these enemies, try to be aware of how they might be operating in your own life. By identifying and understanding these obstacles, you can begin to overcome them and step into the fullness of who God has called you to be.

Competition

One of the enemy's tactics is to make you compare yourself to others, creating feelings of inadequacy and self-doubt. There have been times when I found myself looking at others who were doing similar work and wondered if I measured up. This comparison trap can paralyze you and make you question your worth and the validity of your calling.

Even the disciples faced competition. They saw someone casting out demons and questioned his authority because he wasn't part of their group. Jesus's response was clear: *If they are not against us, they are for us* (Mark 9:40). This teaches us that those working towards the same divine purpose are your allies, not your competitors.

When I see others doing similar work, my mindset has shifted from one of competition to one of collaboration. I realize that if God is calling multiple people to the same mission, it must be significant to His heart. This understanding encourages me and reaffirms the importance of my work.

For instance, at the core of *Brand with Grace* is the need to understand identity. God emphasized to me that His people must grasp their inheritance and unique identity. When I encounter others with similar revelations, it confirms that this message is vital. Instead of feeling threatened, I feel empowered knowing that God is working through many of us to spread His truth.

Instead of retreating when I see others doing similar work, I embrace it. I seek out these individuals, learn from them, and support them. For example, a participant in our Brand with Grace Identity Immersion Group Experience mentioned another author with a similar message. I bought the book, and my husband and I started reading it together. The similarities were astounding and encouraging, reaffirming that I am on the right path.

Competition: Kenny Glover's Perspective*

In the Kingdom, there shouldn't be any competition; we should all agree with one another, make peace, surrender, aid, and assist one another. For us to do the opposite would be to clash, present conflict, contend, or wrestle with others. This tension makes it difficult to come together and accomplish goals.

———————————

*Kenny Glover, my dear husband

Within the Kingdom of God, people sometimes wrestle with competition. They say, "We're Kingdom." They say, "We're doing it God's way." But in life and business, God has specific ways for His children to accomplish His will—and that includes not copying the world or looking over the fence at others to see their strategies.

God has a storehouse full of wisdom just for you and me. He has amazing grace for you. And what you have to do is seek out and acknowledge Him to understand what that grace is.

It's easy to get caught up in competition, especially in the marketplace, because you can base your success on money. This can lead to a money-mindset that can put you into the competition trap and have you eyeing those who are doing similar things as your "competitors." But we don't have competitors in the Kingdom—we are all allies in the Kingdom of God. We help each other, we aid each other. We assist each other in the Kingdom; we barter to help one another form relationships. We don't have the world's mentality of scarcity and competition.

Even when there are so many different people within your space, God still makes a way for you; there's an area that is reserved only for you. And you have to seek God to find out what that area is. You must be patient and grow with God, who builds slowly. Because when ministries or businesses are built slowly, they are stronger, and they endure. They can go through the storm and the rain and not fall over or sink.

Competition should not hinder your progress. Instead, see it as a sign that you are aligned with God's heart. When you encounter others with the same mission, let it fuel your passion and confirm your calling. Embrace the power of collaboration and draw strength from the community of believers working towards the same goal. By seeking God and His wisdom, you will grow in understanding and live out your unique calling with confidence and peace, free from the constraints of competition and comparison.

Competition in the Bible

Truly God is good to Israel, to those whose hearts are pure. But as for me, I almost lost my footing. My feet were slipping, and I was almost gone. For I envied the proud when I saw them prosper despite their wickedness. They seem to live such painless lives; their bodies are so healthy and strong. They don't have troubles like other people; they're not plagued with problems like everyone else. They wear pride like a jeweled necklace and clothe themselves with cruelty. These fat cats have everything their hearts could ever wish for! (Psalm 73:1-7 NLT)

Asaph is sitting here complaining and talking to God. In the KGV (Kenny Glover Version), he is saying, *Listen, God, these people get everything they want.* In life and business, it looks like people have everything they desire, everything their heart is asking for.

I have personally experienced that sentiment, and sometimes it looks that way. But it's important for you to understand that you shouldn't compete. You shouldn't look over the fence. When God has you in the place where He wants you, you focus on Him.

Let's continue reading in Psalms 73.

They scoff and speak only evil; in their pride, they seek to crush others. They boast against the very heavens, and their words strut throughout the earth. And so the people are dismayed and confused, drinking in all their words. "What does God know?" they ask. "Does the Most High even know what's happening? Look at these wicked people—enjoying a life of ease while their riches multiply. Did I keep my heart pure for nothing? Did I keep myself innocent for no reason?" (Psalm 73:8-13 NLT)

Here's another Kenny Glover commentary on the scripture you just read—we start telling God our woes. *God, did I keep my heart pure for nothing? God, I'm doing all this for You, and still, nothing is happening. And look at the people in my community and the people in my field prospering so quickly. They just got started in business six months ago, and I've been doing this for six years. What's going on, God?* We ask these questions foolishly—we ask these questions because we can't see the result.

> I get nothing but trouble all day long; every morning brings me pain. If I had really spoken this way to others, I would have been a traitor to your people. So I tried to understand why the wicked prosper. But what a difficult task it is! Then I went into your sanctuary, O God, and I finally understood the destiny of the wicked. (Psalm 73:14-17 NLT)

This is how it all begins to make sense—when you go to the sanctuary.

This is where you need to be. You need to be before the face of God, seeking Him, because in His storehouse, He has wisdom that you haven't even touched yet. And He's just waiting for you to get into position so He can give you the information you need, the strategies you need, and the clients and employees you need. You need to draw near to God. You're not like the world. You're not so worldly-driven that you're going to do whatever it takes to "succeed."

That's not how you operate. That's not how you work with grace.

Once Asaph went into the sanctuary, God started to reveal some things to him about the destiny of the wicked.

> Truly, you put them on a slippery path and send them sliding over the cliff to destruction. In an instant they are destroyed, completely swept away by terrors. When you arise, O Lord, you will laugh at their silly ideas as a person laughs at dreams in the morning. Then I realized that my heart was bitter, and I was all torn up inside. (Psalm 73:18-21 NLT)

When you get into the presence of God, you start understanding things about yourself and the Kingdom and the places you're assigned, just as Asaph saw that his heart was bitter. When your heart is bitter, you look at everything else except for God. You don't look up; you look side-to-side and all around. And that means you're looking at people. You're looking at everybody else. But God wants you to look up at Him. Matthew 6:33 says, *Seek ye first the kingdom of God and His righteousness and all these things will be added unto you* (KJV). Whatever you need, He will add it. He will add it because He is faithful to His children and wants to bless you.

Let's get back to the Psalm. As you read in the scripture below, Asaph started to see where he went wrong—and the same goes for you when you begin to see you've been looking everywhere but up. You must understand that you go to God for His strategies and His ideas.

> I was so foolish and ignorant—I must have seemed like a senseless animal to you. Yet I still belong to you; you hold my right hand. You guide me with your counsel, leading me to a glorious destiny. Whom have I in heaven but you?

I desire you more than anything on earth. My health may fail, and my spirit may grow weak, but God remains the strength of my heart; He is mine forever. (Psalm 73:22-26 NLT)

God wants to lead you to your glorious destiny. But you have to seek Him and not look at anyone else as supreme authority. Asaph expressed himself to God, telling Him he desired Him more than anything else. That's how you should be as you continue to fall in love with God more and more each day and as you show Him how much He means to you—by worshiping Him and giving back to Him everything you have.

When you honor God in this way, He rains down His blessings on you—because He sees you with your hands and eyes upward. God picks you up and helps you. That's why it makes no sense to compete with others in God's kingdom.

Those who desert him will perish, for you destroy those who abandon you. But as for me, how good it is to be near God! I have made the Sovereign Lord my shelter, and I will tell everyone about the wonderful things you do. (Psalm 73:27-28 NLT)

Make God your shelter. Make God your everything. Show God how much you care, because He will give these things to you. He will help you and continue to bless you. As His people, don't look to the left or the right—look up to God.

Daniel 1:8-20 tells the story of how Daniel refused to eat the same foods as everyone else. He stood his ground and chose not to defile himself by eating the meat or drinking the wine the king gave him. When you follow the Lord's instruction, you are going to stand out more than others because you're working His way. You're not defiling yourself by following worldly strategies.

In the story of Daniel, the king's attendant realized that Daniel and his friends looked healthier and better nourished than those who had eaten the king's food. He also noticed that God blessed them with an unusual ability to understand literature and wisdom, as well as the ability to interpret dreams and visions. When you trust God's leading for your life, people are going to stop and notice you, too. They'll see a difference in the way you operate in the marketplace and want to emulate your actions and your witness, as you give God glory in all you do in your life and work. God wants everything to flourish within you—in your personal life and in your business.

As you operate your life and business in ways that glorify God, there is no need to compare and compete, because others will see the specific work you do as necessary and useful.

God has a way for you that won't cause you to lose your identity or your vision. You won't look over the fence at someone else. Remember Asaph—he looked over the fence, but he didn't see the big picture. At first, he just saw how much others seemed to prosper and how it looked as if they were getting away with everything while he was keeping his heart pure for nothing. He couldn't see how it would end.

When you're running with God, He will show you how to run the race from start to finish so you will be able to complete it with endurance and patience. Don't compare yourself to others. And keep focusing on God. Because when you do, God will reveal strategies from Heaven and give you everything you need.

Looking over the fence at others can trap you in a cycle of dissatisfaction and envy. When you are constantly comparing yourself to others, you may lose sight of the unique path God has for you. Each person has a distinct journey, and God's plans for you are specific to you alone. Trust in His timing and His ways.

When you focus on your relationship with God and seek His guidance, He will reveal His plans and purposes for you. Spend time in prayer, meditate on His Word, and seek His wisdom. As you do this, you will begin to understand more about your identity in Christ and the unique calling He has placed on your life.

God created you with a specific purpose and a unique identity. Embrace who you are in Christ and trust that He has equipped you with everything you need to fulfill your calling. Instead of looking at others and comparing your journey to theirs, focus on what God has for you. Your path may look different, and that's perfectly fine. God's plans for you are just as significant as His plans for anyone else.

In John 21:22, Jesus said to Peter, "If I want him to remain alive until I return, what is that to you? You must follow me." This scripture reminds us that our focus should be on following Jesus and not on what others are doing. Your journey is between you and God, and it's crucial to keep your eyes on Him.

Psalm 73 serves as a powerful reminder of the dangers of competition and comparison. As Asaph discovered, true understanding and peace come from being in God's presence and seeking His wisdom. When you focus on God and His plans for your life, you will find the strength and guidance you need to succeed without falling into the trap of competition.

Remember, in the Kingdom of God, we are allies, not competitors. We are here to support and uplift each other. By focusing on God and His unique calling for your life, you can avoid the pitfalls of comparison and competition and walk confidently in the identity He has given you.

Practical Steps to Overcome Competition

Pray for Guidance. Ask God to show you others who are called to similar missions. This will help you see them as allies rather than competitors.

Support each other if you are led to. I encourage you to engage with their work, buy their books, attend their events, and encourage them. This builds a sense of community and shared purpose.

Focus on Your Unique Path. Remember that while the mission might be similar, your approach and delivery are unique to you. Trust that God has a distinct plan for how you will fulfill His purpose.

Let's close with a prayer similar to what Paul prayed for the Colossians:

Prayer

Heavenly Father, I ask that You give me complete knowledge of Your will and provide me with spiritual wisdom and understanding. Help me live a life that always honors and pleases

You, and may my life produce every kind of good fruit. As I get to know You better, may I be strengthened with all Your glorious power so I will have all the endurance and patience I need. Fill me with joy, always thanking You for Your goodness. Thank You for rescuing me from the kingdom of darkness and bringing me into the Kingdom of Your dear Son. Amen.

Fear

Another one of the enemy's tactics to steal our identity in God is fear. Fear is an enemy of identity because it stops you from having a vision.

Fear in the Bible

In 2 Chronicles 32, Assyria had invaded Judah, and King Hezekiah was preparing the military because King Sennacherib was coming to attack. He was coming to invade, so Hezekiah called on his military advisors, and they made plans to stop the flow of the spring so the army wouldn't have water. It's also important to note that this was a time when Hezekiah was restoring things to the way they had been and bringing the people back to worship the God of Israel, because there had been evil kings before him that had led the people astray.

King Hezekiah brought alignment back to Judah, but now they were facing a threat, as the King of Assyria, King Sennacherib, told the people that Hezekiah was wrong and that he was going to get them killed. He relentlessly mocked them and tried to stir up fear in their hearts.And Sennacherib's officers further mocked the Lord God and his servant Hezekiah, heaping insult upon insult. The king also sent letters scorning the Lord, the God of Israel. He wrote, "Just as the gods of all the other nations failed to rescue their people from my power, so the God of Hezekiah will also fail." The Assyrian officials who brought the letters shouted this in Hebrew to the people gathered on the walls of the city, trying to terrify them so it would be easier to capture the city. These officers talked about the God of Jerusalem as though he were one of the pagan gods, made by human hands. (2 Chronicles 32:16-19 NLT)

Here we see an example of what the enemy does even today—he talks a lot. He talks loudly. And he does it to try to stir up fear.

In verse 18, notice how the officials are shouting in Hebrew, the people's native dialect. They did this so that not only would the people hear and understand, but hopefully become so afraid that they would be easier to overcome and conquer.

And it's the same thing the enemy does to us today. He'll speak lies against your identity so it'll be easier to defeat you. When you're operating in fear, you don't have protection. You become weak and double-minded because you don't believe what God said.

The tactic of fear the enemy uses against your identity is meant to break you down so that you won't even recognize yourself, and the enemy can come in and make you believe what he's saying about you or what others have said about you; you begin to walk in that lie instead of looking toward the vision God put before you.

But I am here to remind you that what God said about you is who you are.

Remember, to know your true identity, you need to have a

relationship with God. You need to have a revelation of who God is, and then God will begin to show you more about who you are, the person He is continually making you into.

In Matthew 25, in the parable of the talents, we see another example of fear.

> Then the servant with the one bag of silver came and said, "Master, I knew you were a harsh man, harvesting crops you didn't plant and gathering crops you didn't cultivate. I was afraid I would lose your money, so I hid it in the earth. Look, here is your money back." (Matthew 25:24-25 NLT)

Here again, we see an example of someone who is operating in fear. The servant was afraid that he would lose what the master gave him, so he hid it in the earth instead of sowing it.

Let's put it in today's terms as it relates to you and your identity. God gives you an idea. He hands you this amazing concept and starts you off with the first step of the vision that He's giving you—create this business, create this program, create this service or membership. He gives it to you—and you sit on it because you don't believe that you can carry it out; it's just too much for you.

Or you ask God, What is my mandate? God tells you to restore originality and creativity back to the body of believers. But your response back to Him is, Me? Oh, no. Now let me go back over here to this other little room and do this instead, because what You want me to do right now is too big. Certainly, not me. Maybe another time—I'm not quite ready to hold and fulfill this mandate, so let me just bury it until a later time.

But God says, *I called you. I told you who you are, I gave this to you not because I need you to start meditating on it. I need you to actually take it and do something with it, not just hold on to it and keep it in a notebook, not go and ask everyone else about what I said to you. I want you to believe Me. Don't let fear of success, of failure, or of getting it wrong stop you from doing something with what I've given you.*

Fear is an enemy of your identity. It comes against what God gives you. It comes against what God says to you.

I want to expose that fear right now. I want to make sure that you understand the tactic of the enemy trying to confuse you so you can recognize it and stand against it by believing what God says about you, instead.

Invitation

Take some time to sit and acknowledge what things you have buried because of fear and begin to come into a space of re-pentance and ask God to show you what your next step is.

Also, instead of just reading some scripture verses about fear or doing a word study on it, I challenge you to look at areas in the Bible where fear was used as a tactic and note how God overcame it. You can even begin with the passage we looked at earlier in 2 Chronicles 32:16-19. Go back and look at that passage and see how the people of Jerusalem who were on the wall overcame the tactic of fear that the King of the Syrian army was trying to use against Judah.

Prayer

Father God, right now I bind the spirit of fear in my life. Expose every enemy coming against my identity, especially fear. I surrender to who You say I am. Help me flow in understanding and go from revelation to revelation about my calling. In this season, help me show up and not let fear make me hide from You. Let me not believe the enemy's tactic of using fear to conquer my ideas, businesses, or relationships. I bind that spirit in the name of Jesus and thank You for the victory. I will meditate on what You have said about me, have a vision, and stand on it. Whenever fear presents itself, I know where to send it. Thank You for the freedom in understanding the enemy's lies and not letting them affect me. I am victorious over the spirit of fear. In Jesus's name. Amen.

Lack of Wisdom and Revelation

As we continue our journey into understanding identity, we're turning our attention to another enemy of identity: lack of wisdom and revelation. This enemy subtly undermines your growth and hinders you from fully embracing your true kingdom identity and mandate.

Wisdom and revelation are essential for uncovering who God has truly called you to be. Without them, you stumble through life, unable to see yourself as God sees you. As you continue to read, you'll explore how the absence of wisdom and revelation can distort your identity and keep you from walking in your mandate. As you continue to seek God you will receive the wisdom and revelation necessary to live out your true kingdom identity.

Lack of Wisdom and Revelation in the Bible

Consider Simon, who later was called Peter. When Jesus asked Simon who he believed He was, Peter answered, "the Son of God." Jesus replied that flesh and blood did not reveal this to him; God revealed it to him (Matthew 16:17). Once Simon had a revelation of who God was, he then became Peter. If he had allowed fear to come in, he would not have received the truth about who he really was.

You have to receive who you are in every aspect when the enemy is coming against you in battle. You have to stand on who you are and who you know God to be in your life.

Now, let's take a look at the Apostle Paul, who was formerly Saul. Saul was a person who lacked wisdom and revelation. He was well-schooled and had been taught by high priests and rabbis. He was a carrier of worldly knowledge but lacked divine wisdom and revelation. On the road to Damascus, he had an encounter with the Lord. Afterward, he started to learn; he had to be taught, and God began to teach him.

Sometimes, you're a lot like Saul—you need to be taught; a lack of revelation will put you in a place where you don't understand your identity and what you're called to do. You acquire wisdom from the Lord about how important revelation is and begin to understand that it's by revelation that you learn who God has created you to be.

> Anyone with ears to hear must listen to the Spirit and understand what he is saying to the churches. To everyone who is victorious I will give fruit from the tree of life in the paradise of God. (Revelation 2:7 NLT)

In this letter to the church, Jesus is talking about "ears to hear," meaning ears to hear in the Spirit. You can have worldly knowledge or wisdom, but for you to understand what God is saying, you must have spiritual hearing. You need to pray and ask God to help you continuously walk in revelation and have spiritual hearing and sight. You need to walk continuously in the wisdom and revelation of God.

It's something that has to be done intentionally and some-thing you will grow in over time. It's not going to happen instantaneously. The Bible does tell you to ask for wisdom (James 1:5); you can ask God for it, and then, as you continue to ask for wisdom and meditate on it, revelation comes.

Have you ever focused on a passage of scripture, and as you were reading, God highlighted something for you and you began to meditate on it? I had a season where I read John 1 over and over, almost every day for an entire month. Just John chapter 1. And every time I would read that chapter, God would say something else to me about what was in that one passage. The more I read it, the more I came into this place of knowledge and revelation. God honors you when you take the time out to seek Him and His Word.

Paul speaks to the Colossian church:

> So we have not stopped praying for you since we first heard about you. We ask God to give you complete knowledge of his will and to give you spiritual wisdom and understanding. Then the way you live will always honor and please the Lord, and your lives will produce every kind of good fruit. All the while, you will grow as you learn to know God better and better. (Colossians 1:9-10 NLT)

You can see from this passage that wisdom and revelation are progressive. You'll continue to grow as you get to know

God better and better. If you have a lack of wisdom and revelation, it could mean that you're not spending enough time with God. The solution for that is to go to the Father and spend more time with Him so you can grow and know Him better. Remember, the more you know and receive a revelation about who God is, the more you know who you are, what you're called to do, what your kingdom identity is, and who He wants to divinely connect you to.

Paul continues, We also pray that you will be strengthened with all his glorious power so you will have all the endurance and patience you need. May you be filled with joy, always thanking the Father. He has enabled you to share in the inheritance that belongs to his people, who live in the light. For he has rescued us from the kingdom of darkness and transferred us into the Kingdom of his dear Son, who purchased our freedom and forgave our sins. (Colossians 1:11-14 NLT)

How beautiful is that? Who wouldn't want to serve a God like this? Who wouldn't want to get closer to Him? So now, let's close with the same prayer we see Paul praying (below).

Invitation

Read a Proverb a day starting with your current day of the month. Continue until you have read all 31 Proverbs then repeat.

Prayer

God, I thank You for Your goodness. Strengthen me with Your glory and power, so I may endure with patience. Grant me complete knowledge of Your will and bestow upon me spiritual wisdom and understanding. Help me grow in intimacy with You, filling me with joy as I express gratitude in all circumstances. Thank You for granting me a share in the inheritance of Your people who dwell in the light. I praise You for delivering me from the kingdom of darkness, purchasing my freedom, and forgiving my sins. In Jesus's name. (Colossians 1:11-14 NLT) Amen.

False Humility

It's no secret that pride is an abomination to God (Proverbs 16:5). But there is a sneakier, more subtle side of pride that isn't as readily recognized, and it's a big enemy when it comes to our identity in the Lord—false humility.

I wasn't even familiar with this enemy of identity myself until God revealed it to me a few years ago. I asked the Lord several questions about why things were not going as I thought they should or why I had a pattern of not showing up. And He answered me simply, False humility. My immediate response to this newfound insight was DENY, DENY, DENY! I hadn't asked God about my character; surely, I had heard wrong.

I shut God off and turned on Google. I went to the internet and found a comparison of pride, false humility, and true humility. I read it, and it made things worse. Now I could potentially add low self-esteem and people-pleasing to the list. At this point, I was thinking that I didn't even know who I was anymore. I brought my husband in on the mess I had created for myself; I showed him the chart and asked his opinion- about it. I shared what God had spoken in my spirit and how this couldn't be right. And being the loving and supportive husband he is, he agreed with God!

I was horrified! How, after intentionally avoiding pride all these years, had I managed to operate successfully in it? After my pity-party, I began to come to a place of understanding that it is the love of God that corrects us. I moved from DENY to a place of repentance and asked God to show me how to overcome what I'd misunderstood.. God lovingly began to show me areas of my life where false humility reigned, and I began to see the patterns.

Here are a few ways that false humility was working in my life (that you might also recognize in yourself):

- Hiding my gifts and talents
- Operating in areas or roles that I was overqualified for;
- Purchasing courses and programs I never used or completed;
- Viewing my assignment in the ministry and marketplace as too big;
- Inconsistency in how I would show up and serve;
- Keeping silent when I should be talking;
- Building for others when I should be building for myself.

If you think that you are dealing with this same issue, it may show up differently for you. As I stated before, the main objective of false humility is to stop you from operating fully in your identity and coming into your destiny. God will help you see what the root of the issue is for you. For some people, it is a fear of pride that leads to false humility. For me, there were several issues that I traced back to my childhood. By the grace of God, I have been healing from this mindset and have been very intentional about staying victorious. But it is indeed a process.

False humility showed up for me most in the marketplace when I worried about "people coming for me." This is also known as the fear of man. We can say we don't care what others say, but our actions or inability to take action can tell another story. Again, this is a hard truth I had to deal with. God lovingly allowed me to see this from the Word of God and get a perspective that would keep me victorious in this battle.

Long story short, I was trying to do everything I could to avoid persecution. If I didn't show up with this new idea that God gave (that is different from the world's way), then I didn't have to worry about the folks who didn't agree. If people didn't know my gifts and talents, then I didn't have to deal with rejection or being misused.

All of this boils down to persecution. But Mark 10:28-30 lets us know that we cannot avoid persecution. Not if we are living for Christ.

> Then Peter spoke up and said, "Can't you see that we've left everything we had to cling to you?" "Listen to My words," Jesus said. "Anyone who leaves his home behind and chooses Me over children, parents, family, and possessions, all for the sake of the Gospel, it will come back to him a hundred times as much in this lifetime—homes, family, mothers, brothers, sisters, children, possessions—along with persecutions. And in the age to come, he will inherit eternal life." (Mark 10:28-30 TPT)

If you want to be whole, you need to allow God's love and mercy to constantly refine you and pull back the layers. Thank you for allowing me to share this truth and expose false humility. My ability to keep showing up where God grants me authority is key to walking in victory and getting to my destiny.

Invitation

Identify where false humility may be showing up in your life. Once you identify it, create a bank of victory scriptures from the Word of God that you can meditate on to help you overcome.

Prayer

Father God, I ask for your help in understanding who you are and how to walk in step with you. I confess that there have been many times when I didn't seek your heart regarding my daily actions. Forgive me for not coming to you first, for being my own authority. Help me to understand how to approach you, especially when dealing with issues of identity and complacency. Open my heart to more of you and help me believe what you say about me, even when it's hard because of what I see in the physical world. Remind me to look to the unseen, understanding that your perspective is different from mine and often more real than what I perceive.

Hear my heart as I move forward, seeking to understand who I am in you and to reject the lies I've believed. The ultimate lie is that I can be whatever I want, but in truth, I am already who you created me to be. Thank you for hearing my heart and for revealing more of who I am. I appreciate encountering you in both profound and simple ways, through peace and the knowl-edge of your love for me. Thank you, in Jesus's name. Amen.

Chapter 6

Influence

As we delve into the concept of influence, I want to begin by offering some definitions. Influence: The ability to affect others or events. Also, the experience of being affected by someone or something else. As I read through the scriptures about Paul's life, one definition that stood out to me for influence is calling. You can use these terms interchangeably—calling and influence. It's also important to note that we're not just talking about influence in general but about spheres or areas of influence. This refers to specific areas where God uses you, where you see greater power, and where the results of your work are more significant. In the Kingdom, your calling or influence is never separate from God's grace. Wherever He gives you influence, He also gives you a specific grace to operate there.

Influence in the Bible

When thinking of the subject of influence, particularly in the context of being a Christ follower, one of the best stories we can reflect on in the Bible is that of the life of Paul.

There's so much we can learn through his journey—from his beginnings of persecuting Christians, to understanding (by way of revelation) who he was called to serve. And then finally, in his walking out what he was called to do by preaching and teaching to the Jews, as well as to the Gentiles.

When we read through the scriptures around Paul's life, one of the definitions of influence we can see take shape is that of a calling. When God calls us to something or someone, it is because He is giving us power in a particular area of influence.

So again, to use Paul as an example, his specific calling or sphere of influence was the Gentiles.

But the Lord said, "Go, for Saul is my chosen instrument to take my message to the Gentiles and kings, as well as to the people of Israel. And I will show him how much he must suffer for my name's sake." (Acts 9:15-16 TPT)

In this verse, we see that Paul is going to be given insight into his calling or area of influence through another person. These words are God speaking to Ananias as He instructs him about what to tell Paul (who was still Saul at the time).

> A man named Ananias lived there. He was a godly man, deeply devoted to the law, and well-regarded by all the Jews of Damascus. He came and stood beside me and said, 'Brother Saul, regain your sight.' And that very moment I could see him! Then he told me, "The God of our ancestors has chosen you to know his will and to see the Righteous One and hear him speak. For you are to be his witness, telling everyone what you have seen and heard. What are you waiting for? Get up and be baptized. Have your sins washed away by calling on the name of the Lord." (Acts 22:12-16 TPT)

In this passage from Acts 22, we see that Paul did, in fact, receive instructions about his calling from Ananias, but he wasn't told word-for-word what God wanted him to say. God's instructions, conveyed to Ananias were very specific— You will take My message to Gentiles, kings and the people of Israel—while Ananias' message was much broader.

So why is this important?

Because it reinforces the fact that Paul received his calling regarding the Gentiles by revelation directly from the Lord, which we hear him refer to time and time again in the scriptures.

The same is true for you! You will receive your specific area(s) of influence by revelation through the Word of God (revealed by His Holy Spirit) and the personal encounters you have with Him.

> After I returned to Jerusalem, I was praying in the Temple and fell into a trance. I saw a vision of Jesus saying to me, "Hurry! Leave Jerusalem, for the people here, won't accept your testimony about me." "But Lord," I argued, "they certainly know that in every synagogue I imprisoned and beat those who believed in you. And I was in complete agreement when your witness Stephen was killed. I stood by and kept the coats they took off when they stoned him." But the Lord said to me, "Go, for I will send you far away to the Gentiles!" (Acts 22:17-21 NLT)

Paul didn't receive his instructions from the Lord by way of a neat, typed-up letter. He got them while he was in a trance! And now he had a choice about whether or not he was going to acknowledge and receive what he heard from God in that revelation.

Now let's travel over to Galatians 2 where we see Paul talking about this encounter and his calling to the Gentiles.

Fourteen years later I returned to Jerusalem, this time with Barnabas and Titus, my coworkers. God had given me a clear revelation to go and confer with the other apostles concerning the message of grace I was preaching to the non-Jewish people. I spoke privately with those who were viewed as senior leaders of the church. I wanted to make certain that my labor and ministry for the Messiah had not been based on a false understanding of the gospel. (Galatians 2:2 TPT)

They even accepted Titus without demanding that he follow strict Jewish customs before they would receive him as a brother, since he was a Syrian and not a Jew. I met with them privately and confidentially because false "brothers" had been secretly smuggled into the church meetings. They were sent to spy on the wonderful liberty and freedom that we have in Jesus the Anointed One. Their agenda was to bring us back into the legalistic bondage of religion. But you must know that we did not submit to their religious shackles, not even for a moment, so that we might keep the gospel of grace unadulterated for you. Even the most honored and esteemed among the brothers were not able to add anything to my message. Who they are before men makes no difference to me, for God is not impressed by the reputations of men. So they concluded that I was entrusted with taking the gospel to the non-Jewish people just as Peter was entrusted with taking it to the Jews. (Galatians 2:1-7 TPT)

Just as Peter had been anointed to take the Gospel message to the Jewish people, we see Paul confirming that he had received his calling directly from God to take the same message to the Gentiles.

When they all recognized this grace operating in my ministry, James, Peter, and John, the esteemed followers of Jesus, extended to me the warmth of Christian fellowship and honored my calling to minister to the non-Jewish people. (Galatians 2:9 TPT)

In the same way, others will be able to recognize the grace operating in your life when you step into the people and places God has assigned to you.

Not only will your area of influence come directly by revelation like Paul's, but you will also have a special grace in that area so others will be able to see it in operation. Just like the other followers of Jesus were able to see the grace of God on Paul as he operated in his calling, the same is true for you. There will be a visible grace that others will see as you walk out your calling in your particular area of influence.

Knowing and truly understanding that you've been sent to a particular area or group of people will allow you to have a sizable impact and see real transformation happen because you understand that God has given you favor in that area. You can walk into that area with boldness and confidence because that's where His grace and favor are. By now you have heard stories of how severely I harassed and persecuted Christians and did my best to systematically destroy God's church, all because of my radical devotion to the Jewish religion. My zeal and passion for the doctrines of Judaism distinguished me among my people, for I was far more advanced in my religious instruction than others my age.

But then God called me by his grace; and in love, he chose me from my birth to be his. God's grace unveiled his Son in me so that I would proclaim him to the non-Jewish people of the world.

After I had this encounter I kept it a secret for some time, sharing it with no one. And I chose not to run to Jerusalem to try to impress those who had become apostles before me. Instead, I went away into the Arabian Desert for a season until I returned to Damascus, where I had first encountered Jesus. I remained there for three years until I eventually went up to Jerusalem and met the apostle Peter and stayed with him for a couple of weeks so I could get to know him better. The only other apostle I met during that time was James, the Lord's brother. Everything I'm describing to you I confess before God is the absolute truth. (Galatians 1:13-20 TPT)

Just like God chose Paul to be His and called him by His grace and love, He has chosen you and called you in love, too. His grace has unveiled His son in you so you can represent Him to the world and reach others through the marketplace and every sphere He sends you into.

You don't have to impress anyone else, and you don't have to try to walk out your calling in the same way you've seen others do it. Even if they appear to have the same calling as you, the important thing is that you walk it out the way God has told you to do it.

Because when it comes down to it, no one can tell you how to fulfill your purpose other than God. We each have to receive our unique instructions from Him.

But when you do yield to Him for fresh revelation about what He's called you to do and who you are through Him, you will come into a place of uniqueness, authenticity, and originality in what you are called to deliver.

And the more you lean in and do what you're called to do in that area where God has given you grace and love, the more anointing, transformation, and power you will have—

because you are being obedient and doing what He has directed you to do.

Invitation

Ask a close friend or loved one where they think you are most effective. In what areas of your life are they seeing the favor and anointing of God?

Prayer

Father God, I pray that I will be open to receive what You are saying to me about where I have greater levels of influence. I pray, God, that I will operate in that influence boldly and increase as I do all the things You call me into. Lord, I pray that I will get past needing attention and past worrying about what others are saying about what I'm doing. Instead, I'll lean into what You've already revealed to me, because this has been decided by You, God, from before my birth. This is not some new training that I have to do to operate in greatness. This is what I am called for. So I thank you, God, for showing me who I am in You and for showing me that I can operate in these areas where You've given me greater power. In Jesus's name, I pray. Amen.

Chapter 7

Messaging

You are a Prophet. What is Your Message?

You are specifically designed to disseminate a message that you carry from God—a message He has entrusted to you by His grace.

But you may not know what your message is. This is why we have spent time going over how to hear from God, how to receive wisdom and revelation from Him, and how to walk in your true identity—because all of this leads to your message which voices the mandate the Lord has given you to steward.

While God's purpose for you remains unchanged, the messages you convey and the methods you use can evolve. This evolution requires you to remain in constant communion with God, asking, "In this season, what does stewarding my mandate look like? What methods best support my message?" It is crucial to stay aligned with God's guidance as you adapt and grow.

This is exactly why the questions in the *Brand with Grace Journal* are designed the way they are, so you can sit with the Holy Spirit and meditate on how He's specifically guiding you—your passions, what you're driven to read, what you're writing, what irks you, what is constantly on your heart, and what just won't leave your mind. These are clues to the specific assignment God has for you.

Prophets in the Bible are messengers sent by God to speak His voice and oftentimes proclaim His will on earth. But I want you to stop and consider yourself a prophet. I know it may be a stretch, but let's think about it for a moment. You are a prophet for what God has given you because you are carrying the message He's given you to steward. You carry that message, so you are your own prophet.

In fact, most of us who are parents are prophets in our households, too, because we are prophets to our children. God gives us messages that we are to give to our children. And the same is true for the business God has given you—you are responsible to administer that message in the unique way God has called you to, without adding to it in any way. And the only way to do that is to hear what God has said about it and follow Him as He directs you to carry it out.

Messaging in the Bible

Nathan is a prophet in the Bible that prophesied during the reigns of King David and King Solomon. He was also an advisor to King David, and God used Nathan to help David. They had a good relationship.

> After the king had made himself at home, he said to Nathan the prophet, "Look at this: Here I am comfortable in a luxurious palace of cedar and the Chest of the Covenant of God sits under a tent." Nathan told David, "Whatever is on your heart, go and do it; God is with you." (1 Chronicles 17:1-2 MSG)

Remember, Nathan was speaking from a place of relationship. He understood that God was with David, because David was a mighty warrior who couldn't win the battles he fought if it had not been for the Lord. God is the one who made him victorious, and Nathan understood that.

But that night, the word of God came to Nathan, saying, "Go and tell my servant David, This is God's word on the matter: You will not build me a house to live in. Why, I haven't lived in a house from the time I brought up the children of Israel from Egypt till now; I've gone from one tent and makeshift shelter to another. In all my travels with all Israel, did I ever say to any of the leaders I commanded to shepherd Israel, 'Why haven't you built me a house of cedar?' So here is what you are to tell my servant David: The God-of-the-Angel-Armies has this word for you: I took you from the pasture, tagging after sheep, and made you prince over my people Israel. I was with you everywhere you went and mowed your enemies down before you; and now I'm about to make you famous, ranked with the great names on earth. I'm going to set aside a place for my people Israel and plant them there so they'll have their own home and not be knocked around anymore; nor will evil nations afflict them as they always have, even during the days I set judges over my people Israel. And finally, I'm going to conquer all your enemies.

"And now I'm telling you this: God himself will build you a house! When your life is complete and you're buried with your ancestors, then I'll raise up your child to succeed you, a child from your own body, and I'll firmly establish his rule. He will build a house to honor me, and I will guarantee his kingdom's rule forever. I'll be a father to him, and he'll be a son to me. I will never remove my gracious love from him as I did from the one who preceded you. I will set him over my house and my kingdom forever; his throne will always be there, rock solid. Nathan gave David a complete and accurate report of everything he heard and saw in the vision." (1 Chronicles 17:3-15 MSG)

This is an example of the power of releasing the right message. Because initially, Nathan said that David should go and do what was on his heart, adding, *God is with you*. But then God came back to Nathan and said, *This is the word of the Lord.* So Nathan had to go back and give David the specific message God had given him.

Have you ever had to go back? Has God ever had to correct something that you said and direct you back to what He initially wanted you to do?

I think for many of us, the Holy Spirit has had to reroute some things that we decided on our own; but God said, *Hey, that's not quite what I want.* This is exactly why we are sitting with the Holy Spirit now and journaling around messaging—so we can open our hearts to what God is saying concerning what He's called you to do, how he wants you to say it, and what that means for the season you're currently in.

Because seasons are important, too.

Initially, David wanted to build a temple for the Lord right away. But when Nathan brought the word of the Lord to him, God declared that David's son would build Him a temple in another season.

And in the very next verse (verse 16), we see that Nathan gave him an accurate and complete record of everything he heard and saw in the vision God had given him, and the result was that it prompted David to go into the presence of the Lord and pray.

Invitation

David's response to God in 1 Chronicles 17:16-27 is such a beautiful prayer. Choose three different translations and read the entire passage of 1 Chronicles 17 in each one. Notice how David was freed by the accurate and complete message that Nathan delivered from God. And then consider the message that you carry in the marketplace, the message that you carry in life—your mandate—and what God has called you to. And consider the results of releasing that message.

Often, we don't understand what that mandate looks like because it can be different for each person. But I want you to look at David's response to what Nathan said (which was ultimately what God said to him) and how it freed him, even in prayer, to begin to make decrees that honored God, that gave Him glory, and that gave David confidence in what he was called to do. We know that David was a man after God's own heart and he already had a relationship with God; but it was what Nathan said that allowed him to inquire and then understand more about his calling as king.

As you read this passage, consider the thing(s) God is calling you to steward right now in this season and what message He is calling you to steward as a leader.

Prayer
Father God, I bless You and thank You for calling me. I am a prophet in my own right, sharing the messages You've entrusted to me. Grant me more of Your grace to work in excellence. Connect me with those who need to hear my messages, and I will deliver them with boldness. Open my understanding to my

unique messages for this season. In Jesus's name. Amen.

Authentic, Authorized, and Anointed Messaging

Your message comes from your mandate. It is what drives you toward that mandate and helps you to fulfill it. There are three things that your message should proclaim: your message should be authentic, it should be authorized, and it should be anointed.

Authentic Messaging

When it comes to an authentic message, an excellent example in the Bible is that of John the Baptist. He had an authentic message.

> In those days John the Baptist came to the Judean wilderness and began preaching. His message was, "Repent of your sins and turn to God, for the Kingdom of Heaven is near." (Matthew 3:1-2 NLT)

Even though you can probably think of others, particularly today, whose message is the same as John's, it was authentic to him and the calling the Lord put on his life.

Authentic means to not be false or copied. It is specific to what God has called you to do, and it goes hand-in-hand with your mandate.

We see that with John the Baptist, and the same is true for you with your mandate in life and business.

Even though you may see someone else who has the same message as you, it does not mean you have the wrong message. Because although we can get distracted by what we perceive as competition, we are all individuals, and God gives us unique ways to carry the message in our different areas of influence.

Think about it. It's just like what Jesus did with His disciples—He multiplied His message through them. They helped Him carry out the same message to others. When God has something very important to give to the world, He'll use multiple people to get it done. And one of the best things that we can do is to honor the integrity of others who have the same message that we have. That's how we continue to proclaim our authentic message.

Sometimes we'll try to find a way on our own for the message to be original, so we change it. But a message is authentic when it is not false or copied; therefore, anytime we change what the Lord gives us, it becomes perverted—it means we're using something the way it was not intended to be used.

Does that apply to your message in the marketplace? You bet it does—because the moment you try to add a signature to the message God didn't intend for you to add, it becomes false. And the moment you try to imitate other people's work, you are copying theirs.

As we draw close to the Holy Spirit, we receive God's instructions for how He wants us to steward his messages. We want to convey the message God has given us in the way He's designed. We want it to remain authentic because we're not comparing it to others. We're not trying to become famous in our own right, but instead are leaning fully on the Lord.

Authorized Messaging

When you're authorized, there's an urgency to your message. God has authorized you to carry out this message in this season. You have clearance to do so. And when it is time for you to move on it, there is a release that happens. Even if sometimes you may drag your feet.

Believe me, I've been there and done that myself. But God is so faithful to forgive, help, and give another opportunity to get that thing right!

The word the Holy Spirit gave me to describe this aspect of your messaging is weaponized. What a powerful word!

You are weaponized, meaning that you have all the armor you need to go into whatever territory God is calling you into with your message. Isn't that exciting?! You have an authentic message, authorized by God—which means you are weaponized to handle whatever is coming at you, whatever you have to deal with along the way.

Think about John the Baptist. He was weaponized for the wilderness, although his weapons looked a little different than most. But he knew how to draw a crowd with what he carried, because he listened to the Lord and stewarded the authentic message He was given. Repent—that was the message God gave him—so he took it and walked it out in authority, so much so, that people came to him in the wilderness.

He didn't have any social media—no phone, no email, no technology. But he was still busy doing God's business—and that's exactly what happens when we operate how God wants us to. When we learn how to show up boldly, we uncover this message, and we then declare it boldly to whomever God leads us, for whomever the message is intended.

Anointed Messaging

Your message is anointed! Anointing is a manifestation of God's grace on your life and message.

Anointing is that special touch of God's power that accompanies His message. In Luke 4:18-19 (NLT), Jesus quotes Isaiah saying, "The Spirit of the Lord is upon me, for he has anointed me to bring Good News to the poor. He has sent me to proclaim that captives will be released, that the blind will see, that the oppressed will be set free, and that the time of the Lord's favor has come." Jesus was anointed by the Holy Spirit to preach the Gospel and perform miracles. When a message is anointed, it carries the same power to transform lives and bring freedom.

This is why uncovering your authentic message is so important. Remember, it's directly connected to your mandate; you can walk boldly delivering that message, just like John the Baptist did, and have peace about it—because it's what you're anointed to do.

It's also important to note that God may often commission you in more than one area; He may place more on your plate than you expected.

I'm currently stewarding four messages right now! But I'm not overwhelmed by it because I realize the timing of God in this season. Sure, sometimes I drag my feet, but I also know what His priorities are. What I normally suggest for people when they need clarity is to sit with the Holy Spirit and consider some questions (like the ones in the *Brand With Grace Journal*):

- What topics should I speak about consistently?

- What has God called me to share about often?

- What am I led to teach and impart and nurture?

Because these things will continue to come up and they will come up in season.

God is so good; He'll put something on your mind, and you'll respond, "Oh yes, I remember that idea." And God just won't let it go. Then suddenly you'll start getting requests from people who are asking you about that exact thing.

It's not a secret. God doesn't want to keep you in the dark. When He's called you to be His mouthpiece, you will know. So again, make sure you take some time to sit with the Lord and you will find peace about your calling.

You can also ask someone else who's close to you, if that helps. Ask these questions:

What do I talk about all the time? What do I tend to be drawn to? As they answer these questions you will begin to understand the message or messages God is assigning to you. Then begin to pray and ask God for His timing and His priority for delivering those messages.

And don't forget to ask yourself, Is this an authentic message? Is this authorized? Do I feel the sense that God is saying, *Okay, now, go. You're weaponized! You have clearance for it!?* Because these are all clear indications that this is the message you're called to steward.

Invitation

Decree this, My message is Authentic, Authorized, and Anointed!

Prayer

Father God, I thank You so much for allowing me to just sit with the fact that You love me enough to give me specific messages just like You did with John the Baptist. And I'm grateful that You'll set me up in a place and with weapons that I may not understand, but I know that You are going to instruct me how and when to use them. God, I thank You for the message that You've given me, and I pray that I would understand it fully and walk boldly in what You're calling me to do. From whatever I create, from that message, God, I pray that Your anointing flows from what we create together. God, I praise You. I ask for more of Your anointing and more clarity around my messaging. God, thank You. In Jesus's name. Amen.

Mandate, Message, Method

We mentioned mandate earlier in this book but I want to take some time to show you how your mandate, message and method are intertwined.

Here's what I believe:

- You can know how God identifies you and His heart for why you are here. (Mandate)

- You can know the messages God wants you to voice. (Message)

- You can know the best way to steward your message. (Method)

There is freedom in understanding that instead of focusing on a niche, you can understand that you have one Mandate, many Messages, and many Methods.

Your mandate is why you were sent. It's what God has called you to do. Your mandate is continuous.

Your message is what you're saying and to whom, because when you know your message, you know your audience. Your message is the voice of your mandate and is sacred.

Your method is how you serve your message. Your method makes the mission of your message most effective. Your method is dynamic.

It's so important to first focus on messaging, then to clarify where you will show up. Your message needs a voice first, not a platform. Remember, your message is sacred and carries with it the power to transform. It's not what it's housed in that brings transformation.

John the Baptist's Mandate, Message, and Methods

I love the Word of God because it gives us a pattern for what we need. God gives us the vision and the revelation of His Word so that we can apply it practically in our lives. And that is exactly what you're doing here with your identity. You're applying the Word very practically to what you're called to do, in the ways you're called to work it, and in how you show up to steward what He has given you.

Let's look at the birth announcement of one of my favorite people to talk about when it comes to identity, John the Baptist. He will be our example of seeing the pattern of mandate, message and methods lived out in his life.

> All at once an angel of the Lord appeared to him, standing just to the right of the altar of incense. Zechariah was startled and overwhelmed with fear. But the angel reassured him, saying, "Don't be afraid, Zechariah! God is showing grace to you. For I have come to tell you that your prayer for a child has been answered. Your wife, Elizabeth, will bear you a son and you are to name him John. His birth will bring you much joy and gladness. Many will rejoice because of him, and he will be one of the great ones in the sight of God. He will drink no wine or strong drink, but he will be filled with the Holy Spirit even while still in his mother's womb. And he will persuade many in Israel to convert and turn back to the Lord their God. He will go before the Lord as a forerunner, with the same power and anointing as Elijah the prophet." (Luke 1:11-17 TPT)

In this passage from Luke 1, we see that John the Baptist had the same power as Elijah the prophet. And he was anointed from before birth, in the womb. Why? Because of his assignment. The size of the anointing depends on the size of our mandate and the size of our message. Jesus said that there is no one greater than John the Baptist, because his mandate was massive. So no one else will have a mandate like that. John finished because he did what he was called to do. No one else needs to prepare the way because he already did it.

That motivation, that unction you have, the power that propels you forward, should always be from the Holy Spirit. Even though that sounds very simple and basic, it is still important to note, because some might say, "My children are the reason why I'm doing this. I have to support them." Or, "Because people view me this way, now I have this drive to succeed because of what happened to me when I was younger." But whatever defines that for you is the power that will propel you forward and how you will operate. Envy can be a driver; competitiveness can be a driver—these drivers are not of the Holy Spirit.

You need to look back over what motivates and drives you to make sure it is from the Holy Spirit—or you may not have the power to see it all the way through.

People start things and often don't finish them. They get discouraged or something else happens and they quit.

But when you know what God said and you know that you're operating from the Holy Spirit to produce, create, encourage, and inspire through whatever He's called you to do, you will have an unstoppable force guiding you. There is no, *Oh, I started this business and I stopped.* You will have a consistent driver that continues to increase.

He will go before the Lord as a forerunner, with the same power and anointing as Elijah the prophet. He will be instrumental in turning the hearts of the fathers in tenderness back to their children and the hearts of the disobedient back to the wisdom of their righteous fathers. And he will prepare a united people who are ready for the Lord's appearing. (Luke 1:17 TPT)

That is John the Baptist's mandate. So what is his message? **Repent**. That's the message that drove the mandate. He was preaching in the wilderness, telling the people to repent. And his method—what he used to get the message out and how the message reached the people—was driven by the Holy Spirit. God drew the people to him, and he preached and baptized them.

Invitation

Read John 5 and pay attention to what Jesus says about John the Baptist as it relates to what He was called to do. I think you'll find some really good nuggets, and revelations will be uncovered for you about how important it is for you to follow your mandate and to have clarity about what your message is and how you are serving it to those you are called to serve.

Prayer

Father, please guide me if I am still uncertain about my mandate. I pray for clarity to reveal my identity, and for me to discern the order and priority of my messages. Grant me an understanding of the urgency of timing and the assurance that You provide the methods for sharing my message. May I operate in the knowledge of my anointing for my assignments. Thank You, Lord, In Jesus's name. Amen.

Part 3

Continuing to Grow Along the Identity pathway

Chapter 8

Building with Stones

Along the identity pathway, we can expect to receive several stones. Each step of this journey, from Hearing God to now, has been strategic and intentional in gathering these stones. God builds with stones, emphasizing uniqueness and authenticity, while man often builds with bricks—uniform and mass-produced. Building with stones means constructing your life and business according to the pattern that God provides through His specific instructions. Stones represent God-inspired ideas, strategies, innovations, concepts, solutions, tools, and resources. These are divine gifts, inspired by the Holy Spirit, that we use to build whatever God has entrusted us to build.

To ground this concept, let's look at a few scriptures in the bible.

Building in the Bible

There are numerous examples in the Bible of people building various structures. But the first one we are going to look at is an example where we find the people doing the opposite of what God told them to do, in the story of the Tower of Babel (Genesis 11:1-9 NIV).

Now the whole world had one language and a common speech. As people moved eastward, they found a plain in Shinar and settled there. They said to each other, "Come,

let's make bricks and bake them thoroughly." They used brick instead of stone, and tar for mortar. Then they said, "Come, let us build ourselves a city, with a tower that reaches to the heavens so that we may make a name for ourselves; otherwise we will be scattered over the face of the whole earth."

But the Lord came down to see the city and the tower the people were building. The Lord said, "If as one people speaking the same language they have begun to do this, then nothing they plan to do will be impossible for them. Come, let us go down and confuse their language so they will not understand each other."

So the Lord scattered them from there over all the earth, and they stopped building the city. That is why it was called Babel—because there the Lord confused the language of the whole world. From there the Lord scattered them over the face of the whole earth.

In this passage, the people used clay to make bricks, a man-made material. Not only did they build something of their own idea in their own strength (and not God's), but they were also behaving contrary to how God had directed them, because they did not want to spread out over the earth; they wanted to stay together. So they built something that man could marvel at but that God was displeased with. They worked together with their human wisdom and human ingenuity and built something that pleased themselves, but not God. And that's exactly what we want to avoid. Because we are all builders.

BUILDING with STONES

By the grace God has given me, I laid a foundation as a wise builder, and someone else is building on it. But each one should build with care. (1 Corinthians 3:10 NIV)

1 Corinthians 3:10 refers to us as builders or architects (in some translations) and emphasizes the importance of the foundation we lay, as well as what we choose to build on top of that foundation.

In the story of the Tower of Babel, the people decided what foundation to start with—which was disobedience, because they knew they were doing something contrary to what God said—and then they chose to build on top of that. Acting in their own will, they started to build the tower as strong as they could make it. And although it appeared to be an amazing feat, it was not pleasing to the Lord. Because of their actions, God came in, confused their language, and scattered all the people about the earth.

This amazing structure they built ended up not even being worth the time or energy; it was built in disobedience and against God's will.

The same can be said for us if we aren't intentionally aligning to God's plans. It's possible that we can build something that man can marvel at by using our human wisdom and ingenuity—or by learning from someone else's strategy and blueprint who's gone before us—to build it our way. Anything we build that is contrary to what God tells us, is built in disobedience; it's building with man-made "bricks." But we want to build with stone.

Let's look at what God has to say about stone (emphasis mine).

You are coming to Christ, who is the living corner**stone** of God's temple. He was rejected by people, but he was chosen by God for great honor. And you are living **stones** that God is building into his spiritual temple. What's more, you are his holy priests. Through the mediation of Jesus Christ, you offer spiritual sacrifices that please God. As the Scriptures say, "I am placing a corner**stone** in Jerusalem, chosen for great honor, and anyone who trusts in him will never be disgraced." Yes, you who trust him recognize the honor God has given him. But for those who reject him, "The **stone** that the builders rejected has now become the corner**stone**." And "He is the stone that makes people stumble, the rock that makes them fall." They stumble because they do not obey God's word, and so they meet the fate that was planned for them. (1 Peter 2:4-8 NLT)

Christ is the living cornerstone of God's temple, and we are His living stones. But Christ is also a stone that makes people stumble, because they do not obey God's Word. For us, as leaders, God's Word includes the specific building instructions He gives us.

Every time God hands us an instruction, that's a stone. We can choose to accept Him and lay that stone on our foundation—which is Jesus. But if we reject Him, we will stumble. And when we reject what God gives us, we accept the opposite of it; if we reject the cornerstone, that usually means we are accepting the man-made bricks instead and are trying to make it replicate a stone instead of building with the real thing, which is a foundation built by God.

What does God say? What does He say is your mandate? What is your God-given message? Where has He authorized you to work? What does that look like? What transformation does that bring? How can you steward that well?

When we listen to God, respond to Him, and stay in communication with Him, we can get the instructions we need and know what He says about us—which allows us to then lay a solid foundation and build with stones.

> Because of God's grace to me, I have laid the foundation like an expert builder. Now others are building on it. But whoever is building on this foundation must be very care-ful." (1 Corinthians 3:10 NLT)

God's grace qualifies you to build and carry out what God is instructing.

Whatever instructions you have followed from the Lord will help you operate in wisdom and excellence. The NLT trans-lation of this verse says, "I have laid the foundation like an expert builder," while the KJV says, "Like a wise master build-er," and the Passion translation says, "Like a skilled master builder."

> For no one can lay any foundation other than the one we already have—Jesus Christ. (1 Corinthians 3:11 NLT)

We are building on the foundation God has laid—and doing it His way, with integrity. We don't build according to the world; because we have specific instructions from the Lord, and we build according to them.

> Anyone who builds on that foundation may use a variety of materials—gold, silver, jewels, wood, hay, or straw. (1 Corinthians 3:12 NLT)

As we build with the grace of God, we must continually trust God for His instructions and not get ahead of Him, because we want to build on top of the foundation with the material that God is giving. He will give us instruction here, too. He may say, "Go purchase that book" or "Teach your kids this." Or He may say, "I need you to be on Facebook and I need you to do a live video once a week around this topic." That's a stone, your instructions regarding what you're building or stewarding; you're doing what God says.

But remember, you have options, and He has a variety of materials with which you can use to build.

But like verse 13 says—But on the Judgment Day fire will reveal what kind of work each builder has done. Fireproof work has value. And we can see that, because even as leaders in family, ministry, or business, we will deal with all kinds of unforeseen circumstances. But if we've built on the right foundation, we will not fall because we've built with the instructions of God.

Building with stones takes patience, both figuratively and literally. When we think about the construction of a home, it may take longer to build with natural elements like stone; and a manufactured home can be built much faster, but the quality will suffer.

For anything of quality, there is usually a waiting period, and it does take time. But I would rather wait for God to hand me a stone than lay anything else on the foundation, because I trust God and I want to make sure that I'm building with Him. My goal is to follow God's leading in life—so I choose to yield to what He is saying at all times.

And that's a decision you have to make on your own. Are you going to choose the information that is readily accessible to hurry the process along and build in your own strength? Or will you wait on the Lord and receive your instructions from Him?

Information and Revelation are in constant competition. Are you going to choose the information or the revelation? Are you going to choose to swim in the sea of information? Or are you going to wait for a slice of revelation? That little slice of revelation is richer and more beneficial for you than the whole vast sea of information that can and will overwhelm you. Revelation is a work of God's grace—it is Heaven handing you a stone, not you digging up your own bricks.

The information can and will set you on the wrong path and cause you to use that clay and try your best to replicate something that looks like stone, but in the end, is not.

We all have that choice. And my mandate is to help you see that everything you need is in Christ. Everything you need comes from that foundation.

Three Acts Required to be a Consistent Builder

To be a consistent builder, three acts are essential: continuous **willful and obedient surrender**, **continuous faith**, and **continuous grace**.

Willful and Obedient Surrender: Hebrews 3:4 (NLT) says, *For every house has a builder, but the one who built everything is God.* We must recognize God as the ultimate designer and submit to His plans, stewarding what He has given us faithfully.

Continuous Faith: Hebrews 11:33-34 (NLT) speaks of faith's power: *By faith these people overthrew kingdoms, ruled with justice, and received what God had promised them. They shut the mouths of lions, quenched the flames of fire, and escaped death by the edge of the sword. Their weakness was turned to strength. They became strong in battle and put whole armies to flight.*

Continuous Grace: Psalm 127:1 (NLT) reminds us, *Unless the*

Lord builds a house, the work of the builders is wasted. Unless the Lord protects a city, guarding it with sentries will do no good. Continuous grace means allowing God to be the Builder and the Source, even while your hands are on the work. It is His presence and power that make what you build enduring.

The Path of Stones for Kingdom Builders

Recently, by revelation from the Holy Spirit, I outlined what I call the Path of Stones for Kingdom Builders. This pattern helps you understand the progressive steps in building according to God's plan:

- Vision
- Revelation
- Wisdom
- Strategy
- Implementation
- Works
- Provision
- Enduring Wealth

Each step builds on the previous one, starting with a prophetic vision from God. Proverbs 29:18 (NLT) states, "When people do not accept divine guidance, they run wild. But whoever obeys the law is joyful."

Steps in Detail

- Vision: A prophetic insight from God

- Revelation: the unveiling of this vision, often through spiritual insights, the word of God, advisors or dreams

- Wisdom: the interpretation and understanding of the revelation

- Strategy: tractical steps derived from wisdom to achieve the vision

- Implementation: putting the strategy into action

- Works: the tangible results of the implementation

- Provision: the resources and blessings that come from continuing to work your work

- Enduring Wealth: a lasting richness that comes from a righteous life lived in God's will

God has everything you need, and it's all accessible by His grace and your obedience to His instruction. Keep doing this "identity work" and continue to grow in grace as you walk with God.

Invitation

Read Exodus 25-31 and observe how meticulous and specific God is with the building of the Temple. And remember—this is the same God who is speaking to you about what He's calling you to do. Exodus 25:9 says, You must build this Tabernacle and its furnishings exactly according to the pattern I will show you (NLT). God specifically chose the people who would help build and anointed them for their mandate and what He called them to do. He gave them special skills and a specific set of instructions. The Lord is the one who graces and anoints you to build anything He's called you to build. There are specific stones, elements, and details that He has for you, and He wants you to come to Him and inquire about what they are. The pattern comes from Heaven; the blueprint is already there. For you to continuously walk out the plan, you have to go to God to get the information. Because He is the one who has the pattern. Now use the resources and knowledge that you have gathered from reading this book and accepting the invitations. Be sure to spend time journaling with the Holy Spirit and be prepared to build with stones!

Prayer

Father God, I thank You so much for Your revelation, Your love, Your abundance, Your mercy, and Your grace. And I pray for a heart to wait. Thank you for increased revelation of who I am and what I am to build, lead and steward with You, God. I will continue to build with stones and not man-made materials, Father, according to Your instructions. God, Your mind knows far more than I can ever know. So I'll wait for Your instruction. And help me, to be rapidly and radically obedient. Help me to wait for Your specific instructions as You anoint me continuously for my assignment. In Jesus's name. Amen.

About the Author

Tasha Glover is a grace-empowered mentor and Kingdom strategist with a passion for helping believers uncover their true identity in Christ and walk out their God-given mandate. As the founder of Brand with Grace and Tech with Tasha, she has guided entrepreneurs, ministry leaders, professionals, and creatives in building lives, brands, and businesses in alignment with Heaven's blueprint.

For over six years, she has led an intimate community where members dive deep into the truth of who they are and the mandates God has placed on their lives. Through the Brand with Grace Identity Immersion Experience, she has witnessed lives transformed as individuals learn to hear God, embrace their uniqueness, discern their mandate, and boldly walk in the path He has designed—by His grace. This book flows out of those very journeys and distills the patterns she has walked with God and witnessed in others—identity, mandate, message, and methods all rooted in God's empowering grace.

Her own journey—from searching for identity through education and career to discovering her kingdom identity by revelation—has taught her that authenticity isn't just an option; it is the foundation of true influence. Tasha believes that when individuals align their life, work, and message with God's detailed instructions and empowering grace—what she calls walking the identity pathway—they don't merely build projects or platforms; they build a legacy of faith and enduring fruit for generations to come.

When she's not teaching or mentoring, you can find Tasha pouring into her family, leading alongside her husband Kendrick as a branch pastor of Charis Missionary Church or creating resources that empower believers to hear, believe, and obey God—and to build with stones, not bricks.

Identity Immersion Membership Community

Grab the journal that accompanies the book and get greater insight into your journey to uncovering your kingdom identity.

Access to all pre-recorded teachings, workshops, experiences, and encounters.